Fixed Income Attribution

For other titles in the Wiley Finance Series
please see www.wiley.com/finance

Fixed Income Attribution

Andrew Colin

John Wiley & Sons, Ltd

Email (for orders and customer service enquiries): cs-books@wiley.co.uk
Visit our Home Page on www.wileyeurope.com or www.wiley.com

Reprinted July 2006

Other Wiley Editorial Offices

John Wiley & Sons Inc., 111 River Street, Hoboken, NJ 07030, USA

Jossey-Bass, 989 Market Street, San Francisco, CA 94103-1741, USA

Wiley-VCH Verlag GmbH, Boschstr. 12, D-69469 Weinheim, Germany

John Wiley & Sons Australia Ltd, 33 Park Road, Milton, Queensland 4064, Australia

John Wiley & Sons (Asia) Pte Ltd, 2 Clementi Loop #02-01, Jin Xing Distripark, Singapore 129809

John Wiley & Sons Canada Ltd, 22 Worcester Road, Etobicoke, Ontario, Canada M9W 1L1

Wiley also publishes its books in a variety of electronic formats. Some content that appears
in print may not be available in electronic books.

Library of Congress Cataloging-in-Publication Data

Colin, Andrew.
    Fixed income attribution / Andrew Colin.
        p.   cm.
    Includes bibliographical references and index.
    ISBN 0-470-01175-0 (Cloth : alk. paper)
    1. Fixed-income securities.   2. Portfolio management.   3. Rate of return.
    I. Title.
HG4650.C65 2005
332.63'2044—dc22

                                                        2004023806

British Library Cataloguing in Publication Data

A catalogue record for this book is available from the British Library

ISBN-10: 0-470-01175-0 (H/B)
ISBN-13: 978-0-470-01175-1 (H/B)

*This book is dedicated to my wife, Linda
and our children, Thomas and Rachel*

Contents

Preface

C.S. Lewis once remarked, 'People won't write the books I want, so I have to do it for myself'.[1] When I first started working on problems in fixed income attribution in the late 1990s, there was almost nothing published on the subject apart from the occasional research paper and conference presentation. I scoured bookshops and libraries for a good, comprehensive text on the subject, but without success.

In late 2003 I found myself in the final stages of specifying the architecture and mathematical models to be used in a commercial fixed interest attribution system for the StatPro Group. With all the techniques and algorithms at my fingertips, it seemed like a good time to write that book myself; and so here it is.

Fixed income attribution is a technical subject that requires familiarity with a wide range of investment concepts. Yet the underlying ideas are not hard to grasp. In fact, one does not need to understand any of the relevant mathematics to be able to read and interpret an attribution report. The reader simply needs to follow what is meant by curve shifts, credit spread and the like, and to possess an appreciation of the assumptions made in the underlying risk models.

The perspective I have therefore tried to bring to this book is not just that of the theoretician, but also that of somebody who has designed and coded attribution calculation engines, worked with complex benchmarks at the security level, and discussed the needs and requirements for attribution systems with fund managers around the world. I hope that the text has benefited from this broad experience, and that it conveys a useful mixture of the theoretical and the practical. Above all, the book is meant to be *useful*.

While I have not scrimped on mathematical content in the text, the less mathematically inclined reader should be able to follow with relative ease.

Fixed income attribution is still in its infancy. A literature search will show only a handful of papers on the subject in the major journals, and as far as the author is aware this is the first textbook on the subject. As attribution becomes a central part of the investment process, the field will probably develop further. In the meantime, I hope this book will serve to raise the level of knowledge about an important topic in portfolio management, and may perhaps act as a jumping-off point for those with a mandate to begin attribution analysis of fixed income performance returns.

---

[1] R.L. Green, *C.S. Lewis* (London: The Bodley Head, 1963), 9.

WHO IS THIS BOOK MEANT FOR?

- *The fund manager*. This individual is at the cutting edge of investment management. Attribution analysis provides constant information on the success (or otherwise) of investment decisions, and forms a critical part of the investment process.
- *The middle-office manager*, who runs and maintains an attribution system. In doing so, he provides feedback and support for investment decisions. For instance, the attribution system ensures that portfolio restructures do not add new risk, and that existing risk management tools are in place and working correctly.
- *The general manager of the fund*, who makes decisions about the investment technology to use – such as risk management, compliance, and performance and attribution software. While not concerned with the details of the attribution process, this individual needs to know that the systems in place are providing the required results, and that they work together seamlessly.
- *The investment systems manager*, who is purchasing or commissioning a computer system to calculate and monitor investment risk and performance. This individual needs to understand the pros and cons of attribution systems, what they do and how they do it; what the data maintenance and reporting requirements are; and how an attribution capability fits into the firm's overall IT requirements.
- *The marketing manager*, whose job it is to promote the fund in the best possible light. The ability to provide attribution analysis results forms an important and persuasive marketing tool, allowing differentiation between funds at a level beyond what the performance league tables can show. This individual promotes the ability to show the precise source of a fund's returns, providing a major sales advantage over rivals who cannot.
- *The asset allocation consultant*, who is familiar with the returns, risk profile and investment process of a wide range of funds. This individual will recommend which managed funds companies and other institutions with funds to invest should use, and so has considerable influence on the flow of investment capital. It is quite possible that within a few years, asset allocation consultants will not even short-list fund managers without the ability to provide attribution analysis.
- *The informed investor*, who wants to pick the fund that can genuinely add value. They may want the added confidence that a set of attribution analysis reports conveys, showing that money is being made in the areas of the manager's expertise, and is not being lost elsewhere.

Acknowledgements

The ideas in this book have benefited substantially from discussions with colleagues at StatPro and elsewhere. I particularly thank Mathieu Cubilié and Didier Cabon in Paris, Carl Bacon, Michael Gifford and Paul Dentskevitch in London, Chris Maden in Hong Kong, and the front-office team at Suncorp Metway in Brisbane. Bloomberg in New York kindly gave permission for use of their data for illustrations. Any mistakes that remain are, of course, mine.

Andrew Colin
Eudlo, Queensland
September 2004

A Note on Notation

For compactness of notation, I have written several of the performance attribution equations in terms of vectors. Vectors support the dot-product notation, which allows an expression such as

$$R = \sum_{i=1}^{n} a_i r_i$$

to be written as

$$R = \mathbf{a} \cdot \mathbf{r}$$

Part I

Concepts of Attribution

1

Attribution in the Investment Process

1.1 INTRODUCTION

My first exposure to fixed income attribution came when I joined the bond team at a fund manager in Sydney several years ago. The economic forecasts and outlook of the manager's analysts were broadly correct, but the fund was not performing as well as hoped, and this was thought to be due to a complex combination of unfavourable credit movements and unhedged yield curve shifts. 'Of course', I was told, 'to find out what's really going on, we need the ability to do fixed income attribution, but that's much too difficult'.

This statement piqued my curiosity. What was fixed income attribution all about, why was it seen as being so hard, and why weren't fund managers using it? I read some papers, spoke to other managers, and gave a few talks on the subject at conferences. It soon became clear that a fixed income attribution capability was perhaps one of the most pressing unfilled requirements for fund managers – not just in Australia, but world-wide.

Eventually the entrepreneurial bug got the better of me, and I left to set up my own start-up producing attribution software. But the questions are as pertinent now as they were then. What is fixed income attribution, why is it useful, and why isn't it used by everyone involved in interpreting fixed income returns?

1.2 THE PROBLEM

In the investment world, people tend to fall into two categories: the manager and the investor.

- The *manager* is the individual, or group of individuals, who use their skill and knowledge to make investment decisions – in other words, to manage other people's money. Managers are paid a management fee, which is often a proportion of funds under management.
- The *investor* decides which managers will look after their money. Investors may not have the same background as managers, but are always looking for ways to boost returns. An *asset consultant* is a particular type of investor, who is familiar with the skills and performance of a large number of managers and will, for a fee, recommend those that match a specified mixture of risks and returns.

Now consider the following two situations.

1. *The manager*. You're a fund manager who invests in bonds. A year ago you hired a star team of economists, credit analysts and traders, all of whom give you presentation after presentation to tell you that their predictions have worked out, just as they forecast. Yet the performance of your fund remains stubbornly sub-par. Something is going wrong, but it's not clear what the problem is.
2. *The investor*. You've just taken over as CEO of a successful dot.com company, and it's time to work out what to do with your employees' pension fund contributions, which your predecessor kept in used bills under the mattress. You have neither the time nor the expertise

to follow the markets, but the large sums involved suggest that the money should be invested in a liquid, accessible form that will at least keep pace with inflation. This involves finding a professional money manager of some form. And it turns out there are lots of them, all in competition, all hungry for management fees. Which ones should you pick, and how can you justify your decision to the board?

These two situations sum up some of the core problems that currently face managers and investors. They include:

- assessing which managers have the best investment skills;
- how to measure the returns on risks taken;
- hedging away unwanted risk;
- finding and removing reasons for losses.

1.3 ADDING VALUE TO PORTFOLIOS

For some investors, any positive return is sufficient, but this view is becoming rare. At the very least, most investors now want to ensure that their hard-earned funds are invested in vehicles that are at least keeping pace with the rest of the market.

In this context, 'the rest of the market' usually means a *benchmark*. A benchmark portfolio is a standard, published reference set of liquid stocks or bonds intended to reflect the current conditions of the marketplace. For instance, one might compose a benchmark made up of all government-issued liquid AAA securities with maturity more than a year, for a given country. No active investment decisions are taken in deciding on the composition of the benchmark, so its performance does not reflect any particular set of skills. Instead, a set of rules that govern credit rating, liquidity and the like are decided on at the outset, and the benchmark is updated each month with any changes required. The benchmark then represents the behaviour of the market as a whole.

Value is deemed to have been added to a portfolio if it shows higher returns than a pre-determined benchmark portfolio, after including adjustments for cash flows and other potentially distorting effects. In other words, the portfolio *outperformed* if its returns are higher than the rest of the market. Conversely, the portfolio *underperformed* if the investment decisions made by the manager have led to lower returns than the benchmark.

An indexed manager provides investment vehicles that follow, as closely as possible, the exact return of a benchmark. Since no active investment decisions are being taken, the fees for such funds are much lower than their actively managed counterparts, and the investor has a guarantee that the funds will not do worse than the rest of the market.

In principle (and ignoring transaction costs), simply purchasing the same instruments that lie in the benchmark, in identical proportions, will ensure that the performance of this portfolio will be identical to that of the benchmark. In practice, index replication is rather more complex, as it is often impractical to invest in every instrument in a large benchmark, so alternative means of reproducing the benchmark's risk and return profile are used.

Benchmarks form a useful guide to how the market as a whole is performing. If the benchmark rises by 10% over a year, and a managed fund rises by 15%, then the manager of the fund has added 5% to the investor's returns.

Less obviously, if the market falls by 10% and the portfolio falls by 5%, then the manager has still added 5% to the investor's returns. In this instance, a better strategy might have been to put the money in a cash account – but this decision was made by the investor, not the manager.

The difference between the portfolio and benchmark return is called the *active*, or *excess*, *return*.

1.4 SKILL IN INVESTMENT

How can a manager generate positive active returns? There are two ways: *luck* and *skill*. Attribution is largely about telling the difference.

1.4.1 Luck

For 12 years, the *Wall Street Journal* ran a monthly feature in the 'Your Money Matters' column, in which the authors constructed a series of portfolios every six months by throwing darts at a dartboard. The performance of this randomly selected portfolio was then compared against portfolios selected by Wall Street analysts. Careful analysis of the results showed that the professionals in the study could not consistently outperform the dartboard portfolio on a risk-adjusted basis (Liang, 1999).

There is therefore clear evidence that many fund managers, despite earning their living by trading financial instruments, cannot perform better than chance. This is expressed in the efficient markets hypothesis (EMH), a mainstay of academic papers for many years (Elton and Gruber, 1995). When management, transaction and brokerage fees are added in, the net result is that active money management often costs the investor dearly. This is one reason for the rise in popularity of indexed funds.

Yet money continues to flow into managed investment funds at an increasing rate, as population demographics and a rising stock market encourage more people to invest in the markets. For anyone with money invested in the markets, these are worrying findings. Are our hard-earned savings and retirement funds really being frittered away by overpaid fund managers who cannot outperform a dartboard?

1.4.2 Skill

Fortunately, there do exist individuals and institutions who can genuinely, consistently add value to the funds they are paid to manage. Some well-known examples include Warren Buffet, George Soros and Paul Tudor Jones, and there are plenty of others.

How do they do it? In roughly decreasing order of respectability, the techniques this author has seen used include:

- stock picking and research;
- economics and the use of econometric models;
- local knowledge;
- chartism;
- technical analysis and black boxes;
- astrology.

1.5 PICKING THE GOOD FROM THE BAD

For most investors, it is not so much a matter of *how* excess returns are generated, but *who* can generate them. Vast numbers of money management firms exist, all claiming superior skill at investing. How can we pick a firm that can genuinely add value to money under management?

One way is to assess the investment process and the qualifications of the fund's personnel. But a more direct route is via a table of historical performance, showing how much each manager has made or lost over a significant period of time – preferably, at least three to five years. This is a good starting point for making the investment decision, and many companies publish league tables, ranking the performance of various types of manager in order.

An important indicator of investment ability is *consistency*. If a trader's performance was down to luck, then we would not necessarily expect that performance to be replicated over subsequent years. On the other hand, a trader who can show a track record of consistent performance probably has genuine ability. In three and a half years as a floor trader, Tudor Jones reportedly only had one losing month. However, this sort of performance is exceptional – and very hard to replicate.

Yet this isn't the whole story. Even if a manager beats the index over a longer period, can we be sure that it was due to real skill? Outperformance over several years may have been due to a fortuitous combination of investments that did not form part of any rigorously defined investment process. For instance, one year's performance might have come from fortunate currency hedging decisions, while another might have been due to a large futures bet by a junior trader. It's important to know why a fund showed good results. Was it always for the same reasons?

One difficulty with investment performance reports is that, frequently, the level of detail supplied is simply too low. Since the returns are the aggregate of many individual and team decisions, the skill exercised by a good, consistent team may be swamped out in the noise generated by their less fortunate colleagues. We can break return down into sectors, but even this does not properly reflect the investment decisions made.

Another difficulty is that returns can be quoted in a multitude of different ways. A fund that is 'Best over 5 years' and 'Top returns since start of year' can top one league table, but do badly on the 'Best over 3 years' and 'Best equity fund over last four quarters'. It is relatively unusual for funds to top the performance table consistently over time.

Is there a way for performance to be decomposed so as to isolate, or attribute, these sources of return? Instead of looking at performance in terms of externally imposed sectors, can we look at the returns from each type of investment decision made by the manager? For instance, is there a way to analyse the returns in the above example to show that the manager is losing money from credit spread trades, but that they can consistently generate positive returns from interest rate movements? There is, and it's called attribution analysis.

1.6   INSIGHT FROM ATTRIBUTION

Attribution analysis provides answers to questions such as the following.

- How consistently did this manager make returns from their stated areas of expertise?
- How well hedged is the manager against risks they do not manage?

At a deeper level of detail, an attribution capability will answer questions such as the following:

- How much did our stock picking abilities impact on our portfolio's outperformance last year?
- What proportion of last quarter's profit was due to currency movements?
- How much return was generated by credit spreads from our corporate bond portfolio?
- How well were our fixed income portfolios immunized against non-parallel yield curve shifts over the last year?

Attribution therefore provides a *diagnostic* capability for investment performance that can be used by both types of individual manager and the investor. In short, it shows where and how the manager added value to investments.

It's hard to overstate how important this can be in all parts of the investment process. If you have not seen the results of an attribution analysis before, you may be surprised at the unprecedented level of detail that an attribution report provides.

1.7   EXAMPLE

Domestic equity fund managers make two main types of investment decision: stock selection and asset allocation. These are covered in more detail in Chapter 3. Briefly, stock selection is deciding *which* stocks to buy; asset allocation is deciding *how much* of each type of stock to buy. Stock selection and asset allocation decisions are usually made by different areas within a fund management firm, as befits the different nature of the decisions.

If we are looking for an equity manager, it is reasonable to choose one that shows consistent ability to outperform the markets over a number of years. One such manager's annual performance table might read something as in Table 1.1.

This is useful information, but tells us little about the internal processes of the manager and whether they can be consistently replicated in the future. For instance, what if this outperformance was due to one star stock analyst who has just left the firm?

To get the true picture, let's decompose these annual returns into asset allocation and stock selection returns (see Table 1.2).

This tells us a much more interesting story. While the fund's stock selection analysts are clearly doing a good job, the asset allocation decisions are consistently losing money. In this case, one might reasonably question the investment process that is leading to this problem, and decline to invest anything with the fund until asset allocation risk is removed.

The hard part is not in implementing the decision; asset allocation risk can be controlled simply by limiting the amounts invested in each market sector. *The difficulty lies in knowing*

Table 1.1   Sample outperformance by year

Year	Total outperformance (%)
Year 1	0.09
Year 2	0.10
Year 3	0.10
Year 4	0.10
TOTAL	0.39

Table 1.2   Attribution results by year

Year	Asset allocation return (%)	Stock selection return (%)	Total outperformance (%)
Year 1	−0.11	0.20	0.09
Year 2	−0.15	0.25	0.10
Year 3	−0.11	0.21	0.10
Year 4	−0.15	0.25	0.10
TOTAL	−0.52	0.91	0.39

Table 1.3   Revised attribution results by year

Year	Asset allocation return (%)	Stock selection return (%)	Total outperformance (%)
Year 1	0.00	0.20	0.20
Year 2	0.00	0.25	0.25
Year 3	0.00	0.21	0.21
Year 4	0.00	0.25	0.25
TOTAL	0.00	0.91	0.91

that this loss was occurring in the first place. There is no way to tell that asset allocation losses are arising just by looking at the returns of individual stocks or sectors.

With 20–20 hindsight, suppose that the manager had known from the outset that they had poor asset allocation skills. To maximize return, they should simply ensure that the asset allocation of the managed portfolio follows that of the benchmark. In this case, the returns look as in Table 1.3.

The total outperformance has now more than doubled. No longer does the manager spend unnecessary time and effort on making asset allocation decisions. Instead, he concentrates instead on the investment 'sweet spot' of adding value through stock picking. Most importantly, investors are happy, and the funds under management will increase rapidly.

For fixed income portfolios, the situation is much more complex, since there are many more types of investment decision that can be taken to try to generate excess returns. These include:

- high-yield investments;
- duration plays;
- curve reshaping plays;
- riding the yield curve;
- credit shift and credit spread bets.

The huge benefit of attribution analysis is that it allows us to see the results of all these different types of decision, decomposed by source of risk instead of being aggregated into one single figure. Attribution therefore provides an entirely new way of looking at portfolio results.

1.8   LIVING WITHOUT ATTRIBUTION

Performance measurement without attribution resembles driving a car forwards while facing backwards. It is straightforward to tell that something has gone wrong, but it can be extraordinarily difficult to assess just what the problem is.

To give an analogy, think of a managed fund as a racing car, with a high-powered V8 engine, tyres specially suited to the race-track, and computer-controlled fuel management. Unfortunately, the car also has a flat tyre, and two of the spark plugs are disconnected. The driver is being overtaken by his competitors, and knows the car could go faster – but he doesn't know what is helping him and what is hindering him. The overall speed of the car is not enough to tell him. He needs specific information about what's helping him forward and what's holding him back. In short, he needs attribution analysis.

1.9   WHY IS ATTRIBUTION DIFFICULT?

Fixed income attribution is seen as difficult. This has to be the case, otherwise attribution systems would be as widespread as performance software. But why is this so?

From personal experience, I have seen one fund manager who tried three times to build a customized fixed interest attribution system in-house. Each effort failed.

With hindsight, the main reason for the repeated failures was an insufficient critical mass of skills. Development of a successful attribution system requires detailed knowledge of the interplay between a wide range of different fields, including:

- market pricing and risk factors;
- data flow issues;
- mathematical background;
- computing knowledge.

If these factors are spread across a number of different domain experts, communication issues will rapidly bring progress to a halt. Ideally, project development should be carried out by a small group led by an individual in a 'chief surgeon' role, reflecting the surgical team concept for software development (Brooks, 1975). As the fund manager found to its cost, such individuals are rare.

It is not usual, for example, to expect a fixed income analyst to have a detailed understanding of database structure and optimization, nor for a programmer to develop mathematical techniques to replicate benchmark returns. Yet these are precisely the sorts of interaction that need to be understood and planned for in designing a successful attribution system. In addition, issues such as benchmark and security maintenance can be remarkably expensive and complex to manage if not handled in the right way at the outset.

It is only recently that affordable, off-the-shelf attribution systems have become available. This has important implications for the build/buy decision, which we cover later in the book.

1.10   WHAT DOES THIS BOOK NOT COVER?

Attribution is a broad field that grows month by month. For this reason, there are several topics that I have not attempted to cover in this text. They include:

- currency attribution;
- residuals;
- differences in methodology between security and sector-level approaches.

Instead, I have tried to restrict coverage to the purely fixed income areas, with detours via equity attribution where relevant. For more discussion on issues common to all attribution systems, particularly currency and overlay attribution, see Bacon (2004).

1.11   WHAT ARE WE AIMING FOR?

In this book we'll be talking about a range of ideas and mathematical concepts. But it's important not to lose sight of what the topic is all about. In the end, the point of an attribution analysis is, simply, *insight* into how a portfolio's returns are being driven by the manager's decisions.

MEGABANK REPORT CARD JULY 2004		
Subject	Remarks	Grade
Duration forecasting	Excellent, provided 20 bp of return.	A+
Credit forecasting	Neutral, just as desired; we don't want to take bets in this area and the results showed that we didn't.	A
Curve positioning	Needs looking at urgently – lost us 5 bp despite not having taken a view. We could have boosted our returns by 33% without the unintentional curve bets the portfolio had in place, which lost us money. Curve bets are easy to remove with careful hedging.	F
Total return: 15 bp		
Comments: Clearly has strengths in some subjects, but can do better!		

Figure 1.1   Sample report card

From the user's perspective, an attribution system is merely a route to a one-page report, perhaps like a term report card, that might look as in Figure 1.1.

Arguably, this sort of one-page report is the most valuable feedback possible for a fund manager. Returns figures are, of course, vital in showing *how* the fund performed; but attribution figures are just as vital, in showing *why* those returns were reached. To summarize,

- Returns give us information about the fund.
- Attribution gives us insight into the manager.

2

Calculation of Returns

2.1 INTRODUCTION

At the most basic level, attribution analysis is about decomposing returns of securities, sectors and portfolios in ways that add extra insight into the investment process. It is therefore critically important to understand how performance of securities and portfolios is calculated.

In this chapter we set the framework for attribution by showing how to calculate the performance of:

- single assets in the presence of cash flows and coupon payments;
- multiple assets when grouped together by sector or portfolio, and when calculated over time;
- portfolios containing various types of derivatives, while showing some of the pitfalls that await the unwary.

2.2 GETTING IT RIGHT

The case of the Beardstown Ladies Investment Club illustrates the importance of reporting correct investment returns.

From the mid-1980s onwards, the 15 members of the club met once a month in the basement of a church in Beardstown, Illinois to discuss investment strategies and to invest $25 per head each month. The club members had an average age of 70, and used their experience and common sense to choose which stocks to buy for the club's portfolio.

The group came to the notice of the global media when they claimed average portfolio returns in excess of 23% over the period 1984 to 1993. This beat US equity benchmarks by a wide margin, and suggested the members of the club had investment skills to rival the best in the industry. Numerous television, radio and print interviews followed, in which members of the club discussed their investment philosophy. The group's books sold over a million copies, while investment seminars and videos also proved popular with the public. Disney even considered making a movie.

The Beardstown Ladies Investment Club did indeed make money, but not by beating the markets! Following an audit of the club's books by the accounting firm Price Waterhouse for *Chicago Magazine* (Tritsch, 1998), the average annual rate of return for the club from its inception through 1997 was shown to be a rather less spectacular 15.3%. The rate of return from 1984 to 1993 was 9.1%, well below the 15% accumulation return of the overall stock market over the same period.

The reason for the discrepancy was that the group's methodology for calculation of returns was, simply, wrong. The 23% annual return proved to have been generated over a 2-year period, not over 9 years as claimed. Other misreported results, such as including membership dues in the returns, found their way into the reported results. Club members said the error was 'embarrassing'.

The moral of the story is that the ability to calculate the returns on a portfolio, in an accurate and timely manner, is fundamental to the subject of performance and attribution. Without a common methodology for calculation of returns figures, it is impossible to compare the performance of a managed portfolio with the returns of competing investment vehicles in the marketplace. *Unless returns can be calculated and reported accurately, there is no point in carrying out performance attribution.*

Calculation of portfolio returns is not a difficult subject, although it is frequently made to appear so. For the uninitiated, the major conceptual hurdles lie in understanding the approximation assumptions necessary for portfolio performance calculation, why they are necessary, and when they should be applied. This requires in turn an appreciation of past and current technology and pricing limitations.

2.3   RATE OF RETURN

Ask an investor what he understands by a rate of return, and the answer will be something like 'the rate at which an investment accumulates value over time', or 'the amount by which an asset has grown, compared to its starting value'. Mathematically, this suggests

$$\text{RoR}_{[t,t+1]} = \frac{P_{t+1} - P_t}{P_t} \tag{2.1}$$

where $\text{RoR}_{[t,t+1]}$ is the rate of return between times t and $t + 1$, and P_t and P_{t+1} represent the values of the investment at times t and $t + 1$, respectively.

2.4   LINKING PERFORMANCE OVER MULTIPLE INTERVALS

By convention, returns of assets are combined geometrically over time, rather than arithmetically, in order to reflect compound growth of yield-generating assets:

$$R = \prod_t (1 + r_t) - 1 \tag{2.2}$$

2.5   PERFORMANCE OF SINGLE SECURITIES IN THE PRESENCE OF CASH FLOWS

How do we calculate the rate of return of a security where the holding of that security varies over the investment interval? In fact, there are several ways. The first is to derive the overall return from first principles, by calculating the return over each interval between cash flows, and then compounding these returns using Equation (2.2).

For instance, suppose we hold $1 of a stock that rises in value over a month from $1 to $1.10, and then from $1.10 to $1.30 during the subsequent month.

The total return over the two months is given by

$$\frac{\$1.30 - \$1.00}{\$1.00} = 30\%$$

Next, suppose that we double our holdings of the stock at the beginning of the second month. The return for the first month is given by

$$\frac{\$1.10 - \$1.00}{\$1.00} = 10\%$$

and the return over the second month is

$$\frac{\$2.60 - \$2.20}{\$2.20} = 18.18\%$$

Again, compounding these returns gives a total return of 30%. Although the amounts invested have changed, the overall return has not changed.

2.6 PERFORMANCE OF PORTFOLIOS WITHOUT CASH FLOWS

Consider a portfolio containing n securities. Over a given time interval where there are no cash flows, denote the portfolio returns by

$$\mathbf{r}_P = (r_0, r_1, \ldots, r_n) \tag{2.3}$$

where r_i is the return of security i. Over this period, the asset allocations for the portfolio are given by

$$\mathbf{a}_P = (a_1, a_2, \ldots, a_n) \tag{2.4}$$

where

$$\sum_{i=1}^{n} a_i = 1 \tag{2.5}$$

The asset allocation of an instrument is the proportion that security holds within a portfolio. For instance, a bond with a market value of $10MM within a portfolio of $100MM market value has an asset allocation of 10%.

Using this notation, the return of the portfolio is given by

$$R_p = \mathbf{a}_P \cdot \mathbf{r}_P = \sum_i a_i r_i \tag{2.6}$$

We can calculate the return of the benchmark, R_B, in the same way, although the number of securities in the benchmark will probably be much larger than the number in the portfolio. The active return, R_A, is then given by

$$R_A = R_P - R_B \tag{2.7}$$

In the framework described here, Equation (2.5) holds true even when the exposure of a security is negative ($a_i < 0$). We explore the consequences of this later in the chapter.

2.7 PERFORMANCE OF PORTFOLIOS WITH CASH FLOWS

We define a *cash flow* as a portfolio transaction that adjusts the holding of a security. Specifically, a cash flow is the purchase of a new security or a change to the amount currently held. For instance, if a portfolio's holding of a particular bond is reduced from $5.2MM to $3.00MM, there has been a cash flow of −$2.2MM.

Suppose that one of the assets in the portfolio has a single cash flow during the calculation interval. How can we work out the return of the portfolio?

It is straightforward to calculate the return of the asset that has the cash flow, using the techniques in the above sections. Unfortunately, it is often much harder to calculate the return of the portfolio as a whole. The reason is that all other assets in the portfolio must be revalued at the time of the cash flow in order to calculate the performance of the portfolio before and after the cash flow. In fact, every time there is a cash flow, every asset in the portfolio must be revalued.

The reason this is difficult is that it requires much more information to be recorded. Quite often, the precise price of a security may not be available, such as in the case of an illiquid asset or a complex derivative that requires considerable computing power to value. To get round this problem, we next consider the portfolio performance approximation formulae.

2.8   PORTFOLIO CASH FLOW ASSUMPTIONS

The work of Dietz (1966) described some ways to approximate the returns of portfolios for which revaluation data was only infrequently available.

Dietz suggested that, for an interval over which the valuation of a portfolio is only available at the beginning and the end, we can approximate returns by assuming they occur at the start, the middle, or the end of the period. For daily time-weighted returns, these are called the beginning of day, middle of day, and end of day assumptions.[1] The returns for each are calculated as follows:

$$R_{\text{BOD}} = \frac{\text{EMV} - \text{BMV} - \text{CF} + \text{Income}}{\text{BMV}} \tag{2.8}$$

$$R_{\text{MOD}} = \frac{\text{EMV} - \text{BMV} - \text{CF} + \text{Income}}{\text{BMV} + \text{CF}/2} \tag{2.9}$$

$$R_{\text{EOD}} = \frac{\text{EMV} - \text{BMV} - \text{CF} + \text{Income}}{\text{EMV}} \tag{2.10}$$

where *BMV* is the market value of the portfolio at the beginning of the interval, *EMV* the market value of the portfolio at the end of the interval, *CF* the market value of any cash flows generated by trades during the interval, and *Income* the value of any coupons, dividends or other internally generated income.

Depending on which cash flow assumption is used, the calculation of asset allocation should be adjusted as well, as follows:

$$a_i^{\text{BOD}} = \frac{\text{BMV}_i}{\text{TMV}_{\text{BOD}}} \tag{2.11}$$

$$a_i^{\text{MOD}} = \frac{\text{BMV}_i + \text{CF}_i/2}{\text{TMV}_{\text{MOD}}} \tag{2.12}$$

$$a_i^{\text{EOD}} = \frac{\text{EMV}_i}{\text{TMV}_{\text{EOD}}} \tag{2.13}$$

where

$$\text{TMV}_{\text{BOD}} = \sum_i \text{BMV}_i \tag{2.14}$$

$$\text{TMV}_{\text{MOD}} = \sum_i \text{BMV}_i + \text{CF}_i/2 \tag{2.15}$$

$$\text{TMV}_{\text{EOD}} = \sum_i \text{EMV}_i \tag{2.16}$$

---

[1] We refer to 'start of day', but the calculation can refer to other periods, such as weeks, months, etc.

Where daily revaluations are used, these formulae give accurate approximations to the true rate of return. They may be used for individual securities or for the portfolio as a whole.

What are the advantages of the Dietz formulae? Unlike some other methodologies, they allow the distorting effects of cash flows to be minimized, so that we can compare like with like. For instance, it is sometimes possible for an unscrupulous fund manager to adjust the timing of cash flows to the start or end of the month to add a few basis points of performance. This is much harder using a proper time-weighted approximation, which is one of the reasons for its adoption.

The Dietz expressions are, of course, still approximations. The curious feature about calculating performance returns is that we know the exact dollar P/L of the portfolio, but the rate of return of the portfolio is still approximate! The big advantage of moving to daily time-weighted calculations is that it reduces this uncertainty.

There are other ways of calculating return, but most of the investment world appears to be moving towards daily time-weighted rates of return to fulfil compliance requirements with GIPS (Global Investment Performance Standards), and the use of such returns is assumed in the rest of the book.

2.9   EXAMPLE 1

Over a given month, a portfolio contains $10MM of a US Treasury bond and $15MM of an IBM corporate bond. During the month, the portfolio sells out $8MM of its holdings of the IBM bond at a price of $116.000, while the US Treasury bond pays an annual 10% coupon. What is the return of the portfolio over this month?

The prices of the bonds over the interval are as given in Table 2.1. At the start and end of the month, the market values are as given in Tables 2.2 and 2.3.

The portfolio cash flow is the summed market value for any trades, which in this case is $-\$8\text{MM} * \$116/100 = -\$6.84\text{MM}$. The portfolio also has income of $\$10\text{MM} \times 10\% = \$1\text{MM}$.

Using the end of period performance approximation, this gives an overall return of

$$R = \frac{(\$18.25\text{MM} - \$28\text{MM} + \$6.84\text{MM} + \$1\text{MM})}{\$18.25\text{MM}} = -11.01\%$$

For a more accurate approximation, the portfolio should be revalued at the day before and after a cash flow. This is one reason for the move to daily time-weighted performance calculations.

Table 2.1   Market prices over month

Bond prices	US T-bond	IBM bond
Start	$110.000	$114.000
End	$102.000	$115.000

Table 2.2   Start of month valuation

Security	Market value
US T-bond	$10MM* $110.000 / 100 = $11.0MM
IBM bond	$15MM* $114.000 / 100 = $17.1MM
TOTAL	$28.1MM

Table 2.3   End of month valuation

Security	Market value
US T-bond	$10MM* $102.000 / 100 = $10.2MM
IBM bond	$7MM* $115.000 / 100 = $8.05MM
TOTAL	$18.25MM

2.10   PERFORMANCE CONTRIBUTION

The performance contribution is the amount by which the risk or return of an individual security or sector contributes to the risk or return of the whole portfolio. Performance contribution is distinct from performance. For instance, consider the case of a portfolio containing a bond and a swap. The bond makes up 80% of the market value of the portfolio, and the swap makes up the remaining 20%. The performance of the bond over a week is 5%, and the performance of the swap is 20%. Which has contributed more to the overall performance of the portfolio?

The performance of the portfolio as a whole is $0.8 \times 5\% + 0.2 \times 20\% = 4\% + 4\% = 8\%$. Each instrument has contributed an equal amount to the performance of the portfolio, even though the return of the swap was four times that of the bond. This is probably more useful than just knowing the performance of an individual asset. Frequently, highly leveraged instruments that show spectacular performance are given such a small asset allocation in the portfolio that their contribution to performance is negligible.

In general, the performance of a portfolio is given by

$$R = \sum_i a_i r_i \tag{2.17}$$

where a_i and r_i are the asset allocation and return of security i. The performance contribution of security i is therefore given by

$$P_i = a_i r_i \tag{2.18}$$

2.11   BRINGING IT ALL TOGETHER

Suppose we are calculating the performance contributions of a portfolio, using the start of day assumption.

Assuming the beginning of day assumption, Equation (2.8) gives the performance of each asset as

$$r_i = \frac{\text{EMV}_i - \text{BMV}_i - \text{CF}_i + \text{Income}_i}{\text{BMV}_i} \tag{2.19}$$

The asset allocation of each asset is given by

$$a_i = \frac{\text{BMV}_i}{\text{TMV}} \tag{2.20}$$

Combining these together, we get

$$P_i = \frac{\text{BMV}_i}{\text{TMV}} \cdot \frac{\text{EMV}_i - \text{BMV}_i - \text{CF}_i + \text{Income}_i}{\text{BMV}_i} \tag{2.21}$$

Cancelling the BMV terms, this gives

$$P_i = \frac{PL_i}{TMV} \tag{2.22}$$

That is, to arrive at the performance contribution of each asset, all we need to know is the dollar P/L (profit or loss) of the asset over the interval, and the total market value of the portfolio. Although algebraically trivial, this is in fact a most useful result, since it means we can calculate the performance contribution of instruments such as highly leveraged swaps and floating rate agreements (FRAs) without having to calculate individual returns and asset allocations. All we need is the dollar P/L for each instrument, and the total market valuation of the portfolio according to which cash flow assumption we are using.

2.12 THE EFFECTS OF FUTURES ON PERFORMANCE

Futures are an unusual asset class, in that they generate dollar P/L without affecting the total market value of a portfolio. They may easily be included in a performance contribution framework by using the above equations.

2.13 SHORT POSITION

Portfolios containing derivatives are often complicated by the presence of instruments with negative market values, such as swaps and options. How can we handle these in the above framework?

The answer is that, providing we are happy to accept the concept of negative asset allocation, no change at all is necessary.

2.14 EXAMPLE 2: SOME UNUSUAL ASSET ALLOCATIONS

Consider a portfolio containing a swap and a bond. The performance of the portfolio is to be calculated using the start of day cash flow assumption. The valuation of the instruments is as in Table 2.4.

Since there are no cash flows, the return of the portfolio is given by

$$r = \frac{EMV - BMV}{BMV} = \frac{\$150\,000 - \$100\,000}{\$100\,000} = 50\%$$

Now consider the performance and asset allocation of the individual assets. The rates of return for the swap and the bond are, respectively,

$$r_{swap} = \frac{-\$950\,000 - (-\$900\,000)}{-\$900\,000} = 5.555\%$$

Table 2.4 Sample portfolio market valuations and cash flow (i)

Market value	Swap	Bond
MV at time T	−$900 000	$1 000 000
MV at time $T + 1$	−$950 000	$1 100 000
Cash flow	$0	$0

and

$$r_{\text{bond}} = \frac{\$1\,100\,000 - \$1\,000\,000}{\$1\,000\,000} = 10\%$$

The asset allocations a_i are given by

$$a_{\text{swap}} = \frac{-\$900\,000}{(-\$900\,000 + \$1\,000\,000)} = -9$$

and

$$a_{\text{bond}} = \frac{\$1\,000\,000}{(-\$900\,000) + \$1\,000\,000} = 10$$

The total portfolio return is therefore

$$R = 10 \times 10\% - 9 \times 5.555\% = 50\%$$

as required.

The difficulty here lies in interpreting what asset allocation figures mean with an absolute magnitude greater than one, even though their use gives the correct result. In this case, a performance contribution framework is more intuitive.

2.15   EXAMPLE 3: A PATHOLOGICAL CASE

Consider a portfolio containing a swap and a bond. The valuation of the instruments is as in Table 2.5.

The swap has had a cash flow of $50 000 and has an unchanged price. The bond has increased in value by $100 000 but has had no cash flows. The performance of the portfolio is to be calculated using the middle of day cash flow assumption.

The performance of the swap is given by

$$r_{\text{swap}} = \frac{\$25\,000 - (-\$25\,000) - \$50\,000}{-\$25\,000 + \$50\,000/2}$$

This evaluates to 0/0 , which is an undefined quantity.

Consider instead the performance contribution of both assets. The total market value is given by

$$(-\$25\,000) + \$1\,000\,000 + \$50\,000/2 = \$1\,000\,000$$

The dollar P/L for the swap and the bond is zero and $100 000, respectively. The performance contribution of the assets is therefore 0% and 10%, respectively.

Table 2.5   Sample portfolio market valuations and cash flow (ii)

Market value	Swap	Bond
MV at time T	−$25 000	$1 000 000
MV at time $T + 1$	$25 000	$1 100 000
Cash flow	$50 000	$0

Table 2.6   Sample market valuations and cash flow (iii)

Market value	Swap	Bond
MV at time T	−$1 000 000	$1 000 000
MV at time $T + 1$	−$950 000	$1 100 000
Cash flow	$0	$0

The total return of the portfolio is given by

$$\text{BMV} = \$975\,000$$

$$\text{EMV} = \$1\,125\,000$$

$$\text{CF} = \$50\,000$$

$$\text{TMV} = \$975\,000 + \$50\,000/2 = \$1\,000\,000$$

$$R = \frac{\text{EMV} - \text{BMV} - \text{CF}}{\text{TMV}} = 10\%$$

which is the sum of the performance contribution of the individual assets.[2]

2.16   EXAMPLE 4: A PORTFOLIO WITH ZERO MARKET VALUE

Again, consider a portfolio containing a swap and a bond. The valuation of the instruments is as in Table 2.6. The performance of the portfolio is to be calculated using the start of day cash flow assumption.

The swap has a return of −5%, and the bond a return of 10%. However, the total return of the portfolio is undefined since it has zero value at time T.

2.17   GEOMETRIC COMPOUNDING

Consider a portfolio composed of n stocks. There may be cash flows in and out of the portfolio, so that the composition changes over time. For convenience, we assume that any cash flows occur at the end of day.

Let:

a_i^t be the asset allocation of stock i on day t;
$\mathbf{a}_P^t = (a_1^t, a_2^t, \ldots, a_n^t)$ be the asset allocation of the portfolio on day t, where $\sum_i a_i^t = 1$ for all t and $0 \leq a_i^t \leq 1$;
r_i^t be the return of stock i on day t;
$r_P^t = (r_1^t, r_2^t, \ldots, r_n^t)$ be the stock returns of the portfolio on day t.

2.17.1   Stock return

The rate of return of stock i over all t is given by

$$r_i = \left[\prod_t \left(1 + r_i^t\right) \right] - 1 \tag{2.23}$$

---

[2] *Note*: The only case in which this performance contribution framework will cause division by zero errors is when the total holding of the portfolio is zero: see Example 3.

2.17.2   Portfolio return

The rate of return of the portfolio on day t is

$$R_\mathrm{P}^t = \mathbf{a}_\mathrm{P}^t \cdot \mathbf{r}_\mathrm{P}^t = \sum_i a_i^t r_i^t \qquad (2.24)$$

The compounded rate of return of the portfolio over all t is

$$R_\mathrm{P} = \left[\prod_t \left(1 + r_\mathrm{P}^t \right) \right] - 1 \qquad (2.25)$$

2.17.3   Sector return

Define a partition of the universe of stocks, so that each stock is a member of exactly one sector S_j.

The asset allocation for sector S at time t is

$$a_\mathrm{S}^t = \sum_{i \in S} a_i^t \qquad (2.26)$$

so that $\sum_\mathrm{S} a_\mathrm{S}^t = 1$ at all t.

The rate of return of sector S on day t is given by

$$r_\mathrm{S}^t = \sum_{i \in S} a_i^t r_i^t \qquad (2.27)$$

On any given day, we can calculate the portfolio's rate of return from the sector asset allocations and sector returns:

$$r_\mathrm{P}^t = \sum_\mathrm{S} a_\mathrm{S}^t r_\mathrm{S}^t \qquad (2.28)$$

The sector's compounded rate of return is given, as above, by

$$R_\mathrm{S} = \left[\prod_t \left(1 + r_\mathrm{S}^t \right) \right] - 1 \qquad (2.29)$$

Note that we cannot compound stock or sector returns and then combine those returns to calculate an overall portfolio return unless asset allocations are constant during the period of the calculation (or equivalently, there are no cash flows). For, suppose this was not the case. Asset allocation changes will not affect the returns of individual stocks, but will certainly affect the overall return of the portfolio.

2.18   PERFORMANCE FROM SEVERAL SOURCES OF RETURN

The preceding sections have shown how the return of individual securities in a portfolio can be combined to give the overall return of the portfolio. In this section we show how the returns of the various sources of risk for an individual security can be combined.

Suppose that a bond's return is generated exclusively by yield, curve and credit risk (we define these quantities in later chapters). Then, the total return of the security is given by

$$r = r^{\text{yield}} + r^{\text{curve}} + r^{\text{credit}} \tag{2.30}$$

where $r^{\text{yield}}, r^{\text{curve}}, r^{\text{credit}}$ are the return due to yield, curve and credit.

These sub-returns can be aggregated in the same way as ordinary returns. For instance, to calculate the portion of a portfolio's return that is due to curve risk, we can write

$$R_{\text{curve}} = \sum_i a_i r_i^{\text{curve}} \tag{2.31}$$

assuming there are no cash flows over the calculation interval. Similarly, the performance contribution of security i due to credit risk is given by

$$P_i^{\text{credit}} = a_i r_i^{\text{credit}} \tag{2.32}$$

3

Simple Attribution

3.1 INTRODUCTION

This chapter is about equity-style attribution, in which portfolio returns are decomposed into stock selection and asset allocation returns. This is one of the simplest and most general types of attribution. The reason we include it is that, quite frequently, the returns of fixed income portfolios are broken down using a combination of equity-style and fixed income-style attribution. It is therefore important to understand this type of attribution before proceeding to the more complex types shown later on in the book.

The techniques of equity-style attribution are widely used and understood. Although there remain various murky areas, such as the choice between top-down or bottom-up attribution and the meaning of residuals, most equity managers can now expect to see the effects of stock selection and asset allocation decisions in their performance reports.

The situation is not the same for fixed income portfolios. There are various good reasons for this, including the much greater number of types of fixed income instrument, the larger number of sources of risk, and the requirement for pricing mechanisms. This is an unfortunate situation, since fund managers tend to hold greater proportions of their assets in fixed income securities than in equities or indeed any other type of investment vehicle.

Equity-style attribution is not restricted to equities; it could equally well cover other types of security such as bonds, portfolios of trusts and property, or other types of investment such as paintings, fine art or even relatively illiquid investments such as rare postage stamps.

3.2 EQUITY ATTRIBUTION

A fund made up solely of holdings in one share will show returns reflecting the manager's skill in picking that share in preference to another. If you buy a Microsoft share and hold it for a year, and it goes up by 30% while the rest of the market goes up by 20%, then you have added value by exercising *stock selection* skill.

However, very few fund managers only invest in one instrument. For a fund containing more than one share, there are two sets of decisions to be made by the manager that reflect on the fund's return.

The first decision, as above, is the choice of stocks to hold. All else being equal, the manager will try to own the stocks that show the highest expected rate of return. But this immediately raises the question: how much of each stock to buy?

The second decision is therefore that of *asset allocation*, or the choice of what proportions of the total capital should be allocated to which market sectors. For instance, you might believe that technology stocks will outperform over the next quarter, and that mining shares will underperform. Accordingly, you sell out some of your holdings in mining shares and use the cash to buy technology stocks, so that your portfolio is overweight technology stocks with respect to the benchmark. The decision says nothing about which particular technology shares are to be bought; that is part of the stock selection decision.

The definition of market sector is, of course, arbitrary. For convenience, shares are often categorized as lying in various industry sectors such as gold, chemicals or banks. However, an equally valid categorization could be by market capitalization, liquidity or (an extreme case) the managing director's shoe size.

Of course, nobody would deliberately choose to invest in a company on the basis that the MD's shoe size is larger than 10. However, the other two splits are entirely plausible. *The value of the split is in how closely it mirrors the investor's investment process.* That is, attribution should closely follow the investment decisions made by the manager, and provide feedback on how successful (or otherwise) these decisions were.

Equity attribution can only be carried out with reference to a benchmark portfolio. Although we can decompose portfolio performance by sector and by stock, this only gives us the raw performance numbers, and tells us nothing about the performance relative to benchmark, and hence relative to the rest of the industry.

Equity-style attribution can be carried out at a number of levels, from the broadest level of share classification down to returns generated by individual stocks.

If one accepts the tenets of the efficient market hypothesis (or EMH), then there is a large body of theory dating from Sharpe onwards that tells us the correct asset allocations for a portfolio that maximizes return, given the expected returns of the investible universe of assets and their covariances. The topic of risk/reward allocation and the efficient frontier has been covered extensively elsewhere (Elton and Gruber, 1995), and we do not describe the topic in any more detail.

In principle, the asset allocation and stock selection decisions are completely independent. In practice, this is unlikely to be the case. We cover this point in more detail below.

3.3 ADDITIVE ATTRIBUTION

Consider a portfolio and an associated benchmark with investments over n sectors. Over a given time interval where there are no cash flows, denote the portfolio returns by

$$\mathbf{r}_P = \left(r_P^1, r_P^2, \ldots, r_P^n\right) \tag{3.1}$$

and the benchmark returns by

$$\mathbf{r}_B = \left(r_B^1, r_B^2, \ldots, r_B^n\right) \tag{3.2}$$

Over this period, the asset allocations for the portfolio and the benchmark are given by

$$\mathbf{a}_P = \left(a_P^1, a_P^2, \ldots, a_P^n\right) \tag{3.3}$$

$$\mathbf{a}_B = \left(a_B^1, a_B^2, \ldots, a_B^n\right) \tag{3.4}$$

respectively, where

$$\sum_{i=1}^{n} a_P^i = \sum_{i=1}^{n} a_B^i = 1 \tag{3.5}$$

r_P^i, r_B^i are the returns for sector i of the portfolio and the benchmark, respectively, while a_P^i and a_B^i are the corresponding asset allocations.

Using this notation, the return of the portfolio will be

$$R_P = \sum_i a_P^i r_P^i \tag{3.6}$$

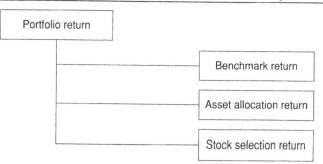

Figure 3.1   Decomposition of portfolio return

and the return of the benchmark will be

$$R_B = \sum_i a_B^i r_B^i \tag{3.7}$$

The active return, R_A, is then given by

$$R_A = R_P - R_B \tag{3.8}$$

Writing active return in terms of asset allocation and stock selection then gives

$$R_P = R_{AA} + R_{SS} + R_B \tag{3.9}$$

as in Figure 3.1.

3.4   BASIC ATTRIBUTION: TOP-DOWN OR BOTTOM-UP?

Consider the processes involved in constructing a new portfolio. Usually, the manager allocates capital to particular market sectors (the asset allocation decision), and then decides which stocks to buy (the stock selection decision). Since the design of such a portfolio proceeds from the strategic investment level down to the tactical level, we refer to this process as *top-down* portfolio design.

The asset allocation decision comes first, so we start by measuring the returns generated by this decision. To do this, we calculate the active weight for each sector, which is equivalent to the difference in sector allocation between portfolio and benchmark. The value added by this decision is then the product of the active weight and the benchmark return for that sector. In vector notation, the value added by this source of risk is

$$R_{AA} = \mathbf{r}_B \cdot (\mathbf{a}_P - \mathbf{a}_B) \tag{3.10}$$

Note that we are using the sector return for the benchmark, not the portfolio. Using $\mathbf{r}_B$ allows us to compare the asset allocation return of the portfolio directly against that of other portfolios using the same benchmark. The only portfolio-dependent variable in the equation is the portfolio asset allocation vector $\mathbf{a}_P$; it is the effect of $\mathbf{a}_P$ versus $\mathbf{a}_B$ that we wish to measure, not the effect of the portfolio's rate of return, and so $\mathbf{r}_P$ is excluded from the calculation.

Given that

$$R_{VA} = R_{AA} + R_{SS} \tag{3.11}$$

$$= \mathbf{a}_P \cdot \mathbf{r}_P - \mathbf{a}_B \cdot \mathbf{r}_B \tag{3.12}$$

a little algebra then shows that

$$R_{SS} = \mathbf{a_P} \cdot (\mathbf{r_P} - \mathbf{r_B}) \qquad (3.13)$$

Next, consider a portfolio that is constructed solely by picking individual stocks, without regard to their overall representation in the portfolio. Although no explicit asset allocation decision has been taken, the implicit effects can be measured. For instance, a fund manager who builds a portfolio composed entirely of desirable communications stocks is taking an implicit bet that the communications sector will rise, relative to the benchmark, and that all others will fall. We refer to this type of portfolio design as *bottom-up*.

When calculating the effect of stock selection performance, we are measuring whether the rate of return of a group of stocks was greater than that of the corresponding stocks from the benchmark. Using the benchmark's asset allocation $\mathbf{a_B}$ to weight these returns allows comparability between different portfolios, and means that the only portfolio-dependent variable is the rate of return $\mathbf{r_P}$. More vector algebra gives us

$$R_{SS} = \mathbf{a_B} \cdot (\mathbf{r_P} - \mathbf{r_B}) \qquad (3.14)$$

which implies

$$R_{AA} = \mathbf{r_P} \cdot (\mathbf{a_P} - \mathbf{a_B}) \qquad (3.15)$$

A third way to calculate attribution returns is given in the frequently cited article by Brinson and Fachler (1985), who work from an alternate set of assumptions to arrive at the following three equations:

$$R_{AA} = \mathbf{r_B} \cdot (\mathbf{a_P} - \mathbf{a_B}) \qquad (3.16)$$
$$R_{SS} = \mathbf{a_B} \cdot (\mathbf{r_P} - \mathbf{r_B}) \qquad (3.17)$$
$$R_{\text{interaction}} = (\mathbf{a_P} - \mathbf{a_B}) \cdot (\mathbf{r_P} - \mathbf{r_B}) \qquad (3.18)$$

The meaning of the interaction term has been hotly debated in the literature on performance measurement (Laker, 2000; Spaulding, 2003a), and it will not be discussed here.

3.5   WHICH ASSUMPTIONS TO USE?

We now have two sets of expressions for asset allocation return, and two for stock selection return, each derived according to how the portfolio was constructed. This shows that equity attribution returns are dependent on the order in which the investment decisions are made, as well as the actual decisions themselves.

At first glance, it might seem reasonable to use Equations (3.10) and (3.14), since both compare the effects of the portfolio management decisions to that of the benchmark. Unfortunately, this assumption is invalid, since it uses the attribution formulae in an inconsistent manner. Combining the returns from these equations together gives

$$\mathbf{r_B} \cdot (\mathbf{a_P} - \mathbf{a_B}) + \mathbf{a_B} \cdot (\mathbf{r_P} - \mathbf{r_B}) = \mathbf{a_P} \cdot \mathbf{r_P} - \mathbf{a_B} \cdot \mathbf{r_B} - (\mathbf{a_P} - \mathbf{a_B})(\mathbf{r_P} - \mathbf{r_B})$$

showing that the sum of these two returns gives the value added to the portfolio, plus an unwanted cross-term effect. To calculate attribution returns correctly, either the top-down formulae or the bottom-up formulae should be used.

Although this is a second-order effect, it can become important where there are large mismatches between portfolio and benchmark sector allocations and rates of return. The reader will often see both sets of formulae quoted in investment performance literature.

In principle, asset allocation and stock selection decisions are completely independent. In practice, this is unlikely to be the case. It is often difficult or impossible to state whether a portfolio was constructed on a true top-down or bottom-up basis, stated process or investment policy notwithstanding. For instance, a portfolio manager's mandate may exclude certain shares or sectors as an *a priori* condition before asset allocation even begins. This makes an unconstrained asset allocation decision relative to the benchmark impossible, so to apply the top-down assumptions is clearly not appropriate. However, the asset allocation decisions were made before any stocks were bought, so we cannot use the bottom-up assumption either.

In practice, the differences are likely to be small unless returns or asset allocation weights diverge widely between portfolio and benchmark. Nevertheless, the assumption in use should always be stated.

If it is really necessary to calculate the attribution returns arising from a combination of investment styles, the two sets of formulae may be combined by using an ad hoc weighting. A 75/25 split in favour of top-down weighting would give

$$R_{AA} = (0.25r_P + 0.75r_B)(a_P - a_B)$$
$$R_{SS} = (0.75a_P + 0.25a_B)(r_P - r_B)$$

Throughout the remainder of this chapter we shall use the top-down assumption, since this reflects the way that most real portfolios are managed. The reader who needs to use the bottom-up assumption can rework the appropriate formulae as an exercise.

3.6 EXAMPLE

Consider a situation where we can invest in four stocks. A benchmark is defined and the stocks show given rates of return over an interval in which there are no cash flows. In the following, we show how to measure the value added by each stock, and by the asset allocation and stock selection decisions.

The four stocks show rates of return as follows:

$$r = (-2\%, 4\%, 1\%, 2\%)$$

Asset allocations for the portfolio and the benchmark are, respectively,

$$a_P = (0, 0.5, 0.5, 0)$$
$$a_B = (0.2, 0.2, 0.3, 0.3)$$

3.6.1 Measuring overall investment performance

From Equations (3.6) and (3.7), the rates of return for the portfolio and benchmark over this period are given by

$$R_P = (0.5 \times 4\%) + (0.5 \times 1\%) = 2.5\%$$

and

$$R_B = (0.2 \times -2\%) + (0.2 \times 4\%) + (0.3 \times 1\%) + (0.3 \times 2\%) = 1.3\%$$

The portfolio has therefore outperformed the benchmark by an amount we call the management effect, M_E, given by

$$M_E = 2.5\% - 1.3\% = 1.2\%$$

How much of this outperformance was due to the asset allocation decision, and how much was due to stock selection?

3.7   ATTRIBUTION AT THE SECTOR LEVEL

Suppose now that the four stocks fall into two categories, 1 and 2. The first and second stocks are in category 1 and the third and fourth lie in category 2. Let's calculate the asset allocation and stock selection returns for the portfolio.

First of all, we work out the asset allocations and the rates of return for the portfolio and the benchmark, when summarized by sector. These are as follows:

$$\mathbf{a}_P = (0 + 0.5, 0.5 + 0) = (0.5, 0.5)$$
$$\mathbf{a}_B = (0.2 + 0.2, 0.3 + 0.3) = (0.4, 0.6)$$
$$\mathbf{r}_P = ([0 \times -2\% + 0.5 \times 4\%]/0.5, [0.5 \times 1\% + 0 \times 2\%]/0.5) = (4\%, 1\%)$$
$$\mathbf{r}_B = ([0.2 \times -2\% + 0.2 \times 4\%]/0.4, [0.3 \times 1\% + 0.3 \times 2\%]/0.6) = (1.0\%, 1.5\%)$$

Using the top-down attribution expressions in (3.10) and (3.13) for both sectors gives the results in Table 3.1. This table allows us to examine the total value added by sector, by asset allocation or by stock selection.

Let's repeat this calculation using the bottom-up attribution expressions. This time, we have the results in Table 3.2.

Most real portfolios do have cash flows of one type or another, and in order to calculate the portfolio's performance we have to be able to compound the portfolio returns. As we will see, this presents no problems when considering the performance of the portfolio as a whole. However, compounding the performance of the various risk sectors can lead to difficulties.

Table 3.1   Attribution results using top-down attribution

Top-down attribution	Sector 1	Sector 2	TOTAL
AA	$1.0\%^*(0.5 - 0.4) = 0.1\%$	$1.5\%^*(0.5 - 0.6) = -0.15\%$	-0.05%
SS	$0.5\%^*(4\% - 1.0\%) = 1.5\%$	$0.5^*(1\% - 1.5\%) = -0.25\%$	1.25%
TOTAL	1.6%	-0.4%	1.2%

Table 3.2   Attribution results using bottom-up attribution

Bottom-up attribution	Sector 1	Sector 2	TOTAL
AA	$4\%^*(0.5 - 0.4) = 0.4\%$	$1\%^*(0.5 - 0.6) = -0.1\%$	0.3%
SS	$0.4\%^*(4\% - 1.0\%) = 1.2\%$	$0.6^*(1\% - 1.5\%) = -0.3\%$	0.9%
TOTAL	1.6%	-0.4%	1.2%

3.8   ATTRIBUTION FOR SINGLE STOCKS

Presenting portfolio returns in terms of asset allocation return and stock selection return is a well-understood concept for portfolios, but when dealing with individual instruments a different approach is often used.

The reason is that applying the standard attribution formulae to individual stocks gives little new information. The value added by a stock i is given by

$$r_{VA}^i = r_B^i \cdot \left(a_P^i - a_B^i\right) + a_P^i \cdot \left(r_P^i - r_B^i\right)$$

When there are no cash flows and instruments are priced consistently across portfolio and benchmark, the stock's return is the same in the portfolio as in the benchmark, in which case

$$r_P^i = r_B^i$$

which implies

$$r_{VA}^i = r_B^i \cdot \left(a_P^i - a_B^i\right)$$

That is, the value added by stock i is just the asset allocation return for the stock.

When presenting stock-level attribution returns, it can be convenient to show the figures in terms of *active return* and *active weight*.

Active return is the difference between the return of a stock and the return of the underlying benchmark. A stock that outperforms the benchmark is said to have positive active return.

Active weight is the asset allocation of a stock in the managed portfolio, minus its asset allocation in the benchmark. A stock that is over-represented in a portfolio, relative to its benchmark, is said to have a positive active weight.

Using these concepts, we can now show intuitively the manner in which a stock adds or subtracts value from a portfolio. A stock can add value by outperforming the benchmark and having a positive active weight in a portfolio. Similarly, value can be added when the stock underperforms the benchmark if the active weight is negative – that is, if the managed portfolio is underweight the more poorly performing stocks. This behaviour is summarized in Table 3.3.

The standard attribution concepts may be amended to represent stock returns in terms of active weight and return. Assuming the top-down model, and working at the security level, the value added to a portfolio is given by

$$r_{VA} = r_{AA} = \mathbf{r}_B \cdot (\mathbf{a}_P - \mathbf{a}_B)$$

The stock selection term is zero for the reasons discussed above.

Suppose we add a constant to each component of $\mathbf{r}_B$, and calculate a new return $\mathbf{r}_{VA}'$ given by

$$r_{VA}' = (r_B + \alpha \mathbf{i}) \cdot (\mathbf{a}_P - \mathbf{a}_B)$$

Table 3.3   Relation between active weight and active return

Active weight	Active return	Result
Positive	Positive	Value added
Positive	Negative	Value lost
Negative	Positive	Value lost
Negative	Negative	Value added

where α is a constant and $\mathbf{i} = (1, 1, 1, \ldots, 1)$.

Then

$$r'_{\mathrm{VA}} = r_{\mathrm{VA}} + \alpha \mathbf{i} \cdot (\mathbf{a_P} - \mathbf{a_B})$$
$$= r_{\mathrm{VA}} + \alpha \sum_i a_P^i - \alpha \sum_i a_B^i$$

Since

$$\sum_i a_P^i = \sum_i a_B^i = 1$$

we have that

$$r'_{\mathrm{VA}} = r_{\mathrm{VA}}$$

That is, the overall value added by stocks to a portfolio is unchanged if we add or subtract a constant value to each component of $\mathbf{r_B}$.

We are therefore free to take any value we like for α. Setting $\alpha = -R_P$ gives

$$r_{\mathrm{VA}} = (\mathbf{r_B} - \mathbf{i} R_P) \cdot (\mathbf{a_P} - \mathbf{a_B})$$

On a stock-by-stock level, this implies

$$r_{\mathrm{VA}}^i = \left(r_B^i - R_P \right) \cdot \left(a_P^i - a_B^i \right)$$

The first term in this equation measures the amount by which the return of stock i exceeded the return of the benchmark portfolio. The second term measures by how much this stock was over- or underweight relative to the benchmark's asset allocation. The first term may therefore be interpreted as the active return, and the second as the active weight.

Remember that this relationship only holds over intervals where there are no cash flows, and for which the asset allocations of portfolio and benchmark hold constant. Of course, this is seldom the case for most realistic intervals. However, it is still of interest to display the active weights and returns for all stocks as a rough guide to the source of stock returns, as long as the results are interpreted in light of the above remarks.

The value added by a particular stock can be measured by considering whether the portfolio was overexposed or underexposed to that stock, compared to the benchmark, and whether the stock outperformed or underperformed the benchmark. Being overweight an outperforming stock will add value, as will being underweight an underperforming stock. Conversely, being overweight an underperforming stock, or underweight an overperforming stock, will lose value.

We can measure the effect of each stock in our sample portfolio on overall value added or removed. The *active weight* of each stock is the weight of each stock, relative to its weighting in the benchmark:

$$\mathbf{W_A} = (0 - 0.2, 0.5 - 0.2, 0.5 - 0.3, 0 - 0.3)$$
$$= (-0.2, 0.3, 0.2, -0.3)$$

The *active return* of each stock is simply the difference between the stock's performance and the benchmark's performance:

$$\mathbf{R_A} = (-2\% - 1.5\%, 4\% - 1.5\%, 1\% - 1.5\%, 2\% - 1.5\%)$$
$$= (-3.5\%, 2.5\%, -0.5\%, 0.5\%)$$

The value added by each stock is then the product of that stock's active weight and active return:

$$\mathbf{V}_A = (-0.2 \times -3.5\%, 0.3 \times 2.5\%, 0.2 \times -0.5\%, -0.3 \times 0.5\%)$$
$$= (0.70\%, 0.75\%, -0.10\%, -0.15\%)$$

In this case, the holdings of the first and second stocks have added value, while the third and fourth have lost value. The overall value added to the portfolio is simply calculated by adding the value added by each individual stock:

$$M_E = 0.70\% + 0.75\% - 0.10\% - 0.15\%$$
$$= 1.2\%$$

3.9 COMBINING ATTRIBUTION RETURNS OVER TIME

From Equation (3.8), the performance of a portfolio can be broken down into benchmark return and active return. We can set

$$R_P^1 = R_B^1 + R_A^1$$
$$R_P^2 = R_B^2 + R_A^2$$

to be the return of the portfolio over two time periods. Combining these returns geometrically gives the cumulative return R as

$$R = \left(1 + R_P^1\right)\left(1 + R_P^2\right) - 1$$
$$= \left(R_B^1 + R_B^2 + R_B^1 R_B^2\right) + \left(R_A^1 + R_A^2 + R_A^1 R_A^2\right) + R_B^1 R_A^2 + R_A^2 R_B^1 \qquad (3.19)$$

But this return is different from that calculated by aggregating the returns due to each sector, and then adding:

$$R = \left(1 + R_P^1\right)\left(1 + R_P^2\right) + \left(1 + R_B^1\right)\left(1 + R_B^2\right) - 2$$
$$= \left(R_B^1 + R_B^2 + R_B^1 R_B^2\right) + \left(R_M^1 + R_M^2 + R_M^1 R_M^2\right) \qquad (3.20)$$

The expressions for return differ in the presence of the last two terms in Equation (3.19), which are known variously as cross-product or interaction returns. These returns are not directly attributable to any one source of risk.

This would not be so bad if residuals were always small enough to be discounted, but unfortunately this is not always the case. If the size of a residual grows to exceed that of a measured source of risk, the results of an attribution analysis can be rendered inconclusive.

Many attribution schemes arbitrarily assign residual returns to management risk returns, using a weighting scheme. However, this is an entirely ad hoc procedure for which the theoretical justification is unclear.

Various schemes have been devised to link attribution returns over time, and a good overview is given in chapters 7 and 8 of Spaulding (2003b). We note that, as yet, there is no generally accepted (or indeed totally satisfactory) means of linking attribution returns, although interesting approaches are given in Singer et al. (1998), Cariño (2002) and Frongello (2002). Two linking algorithms used in commercially available systems were published in Bonafede et al. (2002) and Cariño (1999).

3.10 SELF-CONSISTENCY ACROSS TIME

Cross-product terms would not appear if we aggregated returns over time in the same way that we do over risk sector. Is this possible?

Adding returns is simple, but does not fit with current ideas on calculating return over time. One answer, therefore, is to redefine how asset allocation and stock selection returns are calculated, so they can be geometrically aggregated.

Burnie *et al.* (1998) present a method for calculating asset allocation and stock selection return that can be geometrically aggregated over time. Here, we present a précis of the main ideas.

An alternative way to decompose active return is to write

$$(1 + R_P) = (1 + R_B)(1 + r_{AA})(1 + r_{SS}) \qquad (3.21)$$

where:
R_P is the overall portfolio return;
R_B is the benchmark return;
r_{AA} is the return due to asset allocation;
r_{SS} is the return due to stock selection.

Since

$$R_P = \mathbf{a}_P \cdot \mathbf{r}_P$$

and

$$R_B = \mathbf{a}_B \cdot \mathbf{r}_B$$

we have

$$1 + r_{AA+BM} = (1 + R_B)(1 + r_{AA})$$

implying

$$r_{AA} = \left(\frac{1 + \mathbf{a}_P \cdot \mathbf{r}_B}{1 + R_B} \right) - 1 \qquad (3.22)$$

Substituting this result back into Equation (3.21), a little algebra gives

$$r_{SS} = \left(\frac{1 + R_P}{1 + \mathbf{a}_P \cdot \mathbf{r}_B} \right) - 1 \qquad (3.23)$$

The management effect for a portfolio has been decomposed into two sub-components of return: asset allocation and stock selection. This calculation is entirely geometric and there is no unattributed or residual return. However, the scheme has the (minor) disadvantage that attribution returns can no longer be combined additively.

At this point we need to justify the use of Equation (3.22) for asset allocation returns. The form of this equation is explicitly *top-down*. That is, it assumes the asset allocation decision has taken precedence over the selection of individual stocks. Therefore, the asset class weights are used, and the formula measures the effect of over- or underweighting sectors based on their relative performance within the benchmark. Any performance left over is assumed to be due to stock selection effects.

However, this may be quite the reverse of the way the portfolio was constructed. A stock-picking (or *bottom-up*) approach may be completely unconstrained by asset allocation decisions. The returns from stock selection are therefore measured using the relative rates of return of stocks against the portfolio weights. In this case, the formulae for r_{AA} and r_{SS} have a slightly different form.

3.11 SUMMARY

For additive attribution, the management effect for equity portfolios may be measured as follows.

Top-down attribution:

$$R_{AA} = \mathbf{a}_P \cdot \mathbf{r}_B - \mathbf{a}_B \cdot \mathbf{r}_B$$

$$R_{SS} = \mathbf{a}_P \cdot \mathbf{r}_B - \mathbf{a}_P \cdot \mathbf{r}_B$$

Bottom-up attribution:

$$R_{AA} = \mathbf{a}_P \cdot \mathbf{r}_P - \mathbf{a}_B \cdot \mathbf{r}_P$$

$$R_{SS} = \mathbf{a}_B \cdot \mathbf{r}_P - \mathbf{a}_B \cdot \mathbf{r}_B$$

Both sets of expressions satisfy the relation

$$R_{ME} = R_{AA} + R_{SS}$$

For geometric attribution, the management effect may be calculated by

$$r_{AA} = \left(\frac{1 + \mathbf{a}_P \cdot \mathbf{r}_B}{1 + R_B} \right) - 1$$

$$r_{SS} = \left(\frac{1 + R_P}{1 + \mathbf{a}_P \cdot \mathbf{r}_B} \right) - 1$$

and the management effect is then found from

$$1 + R_{ME} = (1 + R_{AA})(1 + R_{SS})$$

Of the two approaches, the second has the advantage that in practice it generates no unattributed, or residual, return.

4

Yield Curves in Attribution

4.1 INTRODUCTION

Yield curves play a major role in fixed income attribution analysis, because movements in yield curves have a large effect on the pricing, and hence the return, of fixed income assets.

A large and complex literature exists on yield curves, reflecting the central part they play in fixed income market pricing. Many hundreds of research papers and several textbooks have been written on their construction and modelling, and yield curve experts continue to devise ever-improved software systems incorporating bootstrap techniques for constructing curves, the dynamics of stochastic interest rate modelling, and sophisticated techniques to match bill strips to bond curves.

Fortunately, it is only necessary to be familiar with a small part of this body of knowledge in order to understand how yield curves are used in attribution. This chapter therefore gives a carefully tailored account of the topic for attribution practitioners. The major points the reader needs to know are how yield curves can be modelled, in terms that reflect their movements in the marketplace. An excellent, in-depth reference to the subject is Choudhry (2004).

For attribution purposes, life is considerably simplified by the wide availability of pre-defined yield curves, and by attribution methodologies that allow the use of curves that are easily constructed from market rates.

4.2 YIELD CURVES

Suppose that you want to borrow $100 for 1 year from a western bank. You have plenty of assets, so your creditworthiness is not an issue. The bank will advertise their loan rate so that you can compare it to that of their rivals. If their interest rate is substantially higher than their rivals, you will go elsewhere, and eventually market pressures will push the bank towards lowering their rate. On the other hand, if their rate is substantially lower than their rivals, they will then have an incentive to raise rates to get higher returns for their shareholders. For all institutions, this *1-year rate* will therefore converge to a market consensus.

The only point at which interest rates are fixed is for overnight deposits, or the cash rate, which is set by central banks. This is the rate at which the central bank will lend money. All other rates are set by the market.

Everything else being equal, should we expect the rate for a 30-year investment to be the same as for a 1-year investment? The answer is: usually not. If a bank lends you money without expecting to see it back for the next 30 years, you (and therefore the bank) are substantially more exposed to downturns in the economy, disasters and the like, during this period. The probability that the cash will be lost is therefore greater. The bank will accordingly want to see a higher return, and the consensus rate will therefore rise, to compensate for this extra risk.

On this basis, we would expect long-term rates to be higher than short-term rates, and in fact this is what usually happens. Assigning higher interest payments for riskier investments is the basis on which credit curves arise (see below).

In fact, interest rates behave in a more complex manner than this. Factors that affect perceived future rates are inflation, the state of the economy, the interest rates of other countries, exchange rates, and many others. For this reason interest rates behave in a wide range of different ways and it is not unknown for long-term rates to fall below short-term rates, or for a range of more complex behaviours to appear.

4.3   WHAT IS A YIELD CURVE?

A yield curve is a graph showing a market consensus of where interest rates are expected to be in the future. Typically, the range of dates lies between today and 20 to 30 years in the future. A yield curve is also known as the term structure, and you will often see the two terms used interchangeably.

The existence of yield curves shows that bond yields do not exist in a vacuum, moving around independently. The yield curve represents the deepest structure of the fixed income market, and the usual market arbitrage mechanisms apply to the level of the curve. For this reason, it makes sense to talk about a single reference curve for a market at a particular time, in the same way as a single exchange rate. When a manager is trading bonds or swaps, it is relatively unusual to consider just one instrument in isolation. If the manager has a view on where prices will go, it is far more likely to be expressed in terms of how the yield curve will move.

4.4   WHY YIELD CURVES MATTER IN ATTRIBUTION

For this reason, yield curve movements are central to the whole subject of fixed income attribution. The majority of fixed income securities have prices that depend intimately on the shape and level of the yield curve across a range of maturities, and so the return of these securities is driven by the yield curve.

This means that management decisions for fixed income portfolios tend to be made in quite different terms to those for equity portfolios.

Equity managers look at the growth prospects for individual stocks and sectors, and at overweighting market sectors that are expected to outperform while underweighting poorly performing sectors.

Fixed income managers, on the other hand, often make investment decisions in terms of expected yield curve movements, not in terms of sector allocations. The manager will look at expected movements in the reference curve – whether it will move up or down, steepen, which parts will move the most – and at movements in other related curves that also affect the pricing, and hence the returns, of the instruments in the portfolio.

For instance, a manager may have positioned his portfolio so that its modified duration is a year less than the modified duration of the benchmark (a year short). This expresses the manager's view that yields will rise across all maturities and so drive down bond prices. In other words, he expects the yield curve to move upwards. By being shorter modified duration relative to the benchmark, the price sensitivity of the portfolio is less than that of the benchmark, so the value of the portfolio will not be as adversely affected as the benchmark, and the relative performance of the two will be in his favour – if he was right.

Since the types of risk in a fixed income portfolio are much more numerous than for an equity portfolio, the numbers of possible strategies are also correspondingly wider – as well as the numbers of ways in which money can be lost! For instance, the manager in the above example has taken a simple duration decision. Even if he was correct, it is entirely possible to lose all the returns made from this decision from other types of yield curve movements, or unfavourable credit shifts.

For all these reasons, a knowledge of yield curves is fundamental to understanding how fixed income markets work.

The construction of yield curves, and forecasting how they behave, are deep and complex areas. Fortunately, neither need be understood in depth when discussing attribution. In fact, you will very likely find that the yield curve data you use in attribution is provided ready-to-go from a data vendor.

4.5   DIFFERENT TYPES OF YIELD

A yield curve plots yield against maturity, but the term 'yield' can have different meanings. For reference, here are the most common usages.

4.5.1   Coupon rate

The coupon rate is the percentage of the face value of the bond that is paid to the owner of that bond each year. For instance, the owner of a $10 000 bond that pays a 10% coupon will receive an annual payment of $1000 until the bond matures, irrespective of changes in the bond's price or yield. A zero-coupon bond does not, as the name implies, pay any coupons, and so the only cash flow is the maturity payment.

4.5.2   Current yield (or running yield)

The current yield of a bond is its coupon, divided by its current market price. For instance, a bond with an 8% coupon that is trading at $110 per $100 face value has a current yield of $8/1.1 = 7.273\%$.

4.5.3   Yield to maturity

The yield to maturity (YTM) is a security's internal rate of return, or the anticipated yield of the bond if held to maturity. The YTM is the rate used when calculating the present value of all cash flows, so that they add up to the current market price. In other words, it is the compounded rate of return that investors receive if the bond is held to maturity and all cash flows are reinvested at the same rate of interest. If r is the current yield to maturity, then a bond's price is given by

$$c(1+r)^{-1} + c(1+r)^{-2} + \cdots + c(1+r)^{-n} + B(1+r)^{-n} = P \qquad (4.1)$$

where:

c is an annual coupon, in dollars;
n is the number of years to maturity;
B is the par value of the bond, in dollars;
P is the current market price of the bond, in dollars.

This equation requires a numerical solution for r, if c, n, B, P are all known. Yield calculators are widely available. Note that this assumes all cash flows are reinvested at the yield to maturity, which is not entirely realistic because the curve is seldom flat.

The YTM takes into account market price, redemption value, coupon and time between interest payments, so it is useful in comparing fixed income investments. Yield to maturity is by far the most commonly used measure of yield of a bond. When we talk about the yield curve, we most commonly mean a graph of yields to maturity plotted against maturity.

4.6   ZERO-COUPON YIELD

The zero-coupon yield of a security is the return it would show if all coupons were stripped out.

For securities that do not pay coupons, such as zero-coupon bonds or bills, there is only one repayment cash flow at maturity. In this case, the yield to maturity is identical to the zero-coupon yield.

For securities that do pay coupons, the price of the security is the sum of the various cash flows making up the bond, where each cash flow is discounted at the appropriate rate for its maturity.

4.7   SOVEREIGN AND CREDIT CURVES

In each market, the most important yield curve is the sovereign yield curve (also referred to as the reference curve, the AAA curve, or just 'the curve'). The sovereign yield curve is constructed from the securities with the highest credit rating, which carry virtually no default risk to the investor. These tend to be bonds issued by a government, that has the ability to levy taxation to ensure their debt commitments are met. This reference curve provides the clearest view of the current term structure, unencumbered by credit effects or other yield curve distortions.

Separate yield curves are associated with each country and currency. Even if securities are issued in different countries but in the same currency, the shape of the yield curve tends to differ across countries. This *country effect* is covered in more detail in Chapter 10.

Credit curves refer to yield curves made up from securities with lower credit ratings. For instance, the AA yield curve for the Australian market is made up of yields from AA-rated bonds.

4.8   WHAT SHOULD A CURVE LOOK LIKE?

From the above discussion, we can put some constraints on how a curve should behave.

- The curve should be smooth, with no glitches or discontinuities. Otherwise, arbitrage opportunities will arise.
- Curves of different credit ratings should not cross or intersect. Otherwise, identical bonds with different repayment risks may show the same yield.
- The curve should intersect the cash rate at zero maturity.

In practice, there can be significant problems in ensuring that curves calculated from raw market data actually have these desirable properties, as we show in the next section.

4.9 DIFFERENT TYPES OF CURVE – ADVANTAGES AND DISADVANTAGES

One problem with constructing curves is that the vast majority of fixed income securities traded in the market pay coupons. For instance, the majority of government bonds pay a coupon once or twice a year, while floating rate notes (FRNs) make regular coupon payments that are calculated as a margin to a market-determined rate.

The presence of these coupons means that market yields are often distorted by the presence of high or low coupons, and this can have a significant effect on the shape of the curve.

A simple solution would be to read yields from instruments that do not pay coupons – so-called zero-coupon bonds. This is practical for the short end of the market, since bank bills and discount securities do not pay coupons, but seldom have a maturity of more than a year. For the long end of the market, zero-coupon instruments are much less liquid and do not give a clear picture of the term structure. One must therefore examine the yields of coupon-bearing instruments to gain a true view of the state of the market.

4.9.1 Par curves

The simplest type of curve is constructed by plotting a curve of yields to maturity for related instruments against time to maturity. This is called the *par curve*.

Constructing a curve in this way has both good and bad points. A good point about a par curve is that it is very simple to build; one selects a set of reference securities, calculates their time to maturity, and plots their current market yields against maturity. No calculations of any kind are needed.

However, a par curve only provides a rough view of the term structure and does not account for the structure of different bonds. For many cases, however, a par curve provides sufficient detail for attribution.

4.9.2 Duration curves

Perhaps the most severe problem of a par curve is that the yield to maturity of each bond is affected by coupon. For instance, two separate bonds maturing on the same day that have different coupons will very likely have different yields. Which one should be used?

This problem is partially solved by using the modified duration of the bond, instead of time to maturity, as the time coordinate for the curve. This modified curve is called the *duration curve*. The duration of a bond is a weighted average time to maturity of the bond's cash flows, and so allows us to partly remove the effect of the coupon.

Unfortunately, there remains the problem that durations change discontinuously over coupon payment periods. As the bond goes ex-interest, the price will drop by approximately the amount of the coupon payment, which leads the bond's duration to increase as the shortest-dated coupon is removed from the weighted average of the cash flows.

Even if duration is smoothed, there can remain difficulties. It is still possible for bonds to have quite different properties but very close modified durations. In this case, the duration curve can still appear to have glitches.

4.9.3 Zero-coupon curves

To completely remove the distorting effect of coupons on yield, we can use a technique called *bootstrapping* to construct a zero-coupon curve that gives a true reflection of the shape of the term structure. This involves calculating the zero-coupon yields of the bonds making up the curve from the actual market yields. The *zero-coupon curve* is then the graph of these zero yields plotted against maturity.

The zero-coupon curve gives the truest view of the marketplace and is the only curve that should be used for pricing, say, a swap's cash flows, or for finding cheap/dear arbitrage opportunities. For this reason, banks running bond arbitrage operations and swap desks spend a great deal of effort in ensuring that their zero-coupon curve models are as accurate as possible, since all their instrument pricing is run from this data. Such a degree of accuracy is probably not needed for attribution purposes, where we are more concerned with the overall effects of *movements* in the curve.

4.10   COMPARING DIFFERENT CURVE TYPES

Does the choice of curve matter when running an attribution analysis? The author's view is: probably not.

The first reason is that, for attribution, we do not particularly need curves at the levels of accuracy required for, say, bond pricing. Instead, what we are interested in is *changes* in the level of the curve, and this is much the same depending on what curve is used. For instance, the change in the 10-year zero rate over a given week will be much the same as the change in the 10-year par rate – even though the absolute values of the yields will be different.

The second reason is that there is a large dose of subjectivity in deciding how a parameterized yield model should be fitted to its underlying curve, and an even larger dose in deciding how curve changes should be broken down into parallel and other motion types. In the face of this, it seems irrational to spend substantial effort in constructing highly accurate zero curves if they will only be used for attribution. Of course, if accurate curves are already available, there is no harm in using them.

4.11   HOW DO YIELD CURVES BEHAVE?

As we mentioned at the beginning of this chapter, the usual shape of a yield curve is positively sloped, rising steadily from short-term yields to long-term yields. Figure 4.1 shows a typical set of curves for the US market over an interval of a year. We analyse these curves in more detail in the next chapter.

However, not all curves show this positive slope. An inverted yield curve has shorter rates higher than longer rates, so the curve slopes downwards. The appearance of an inverted yield curve can be a sign that the market believes a recession is imminent, and the difference between long and short rates gives an indication of how severe the recession will be.

For instance, Figure 4.2 shows the UK government benchmark curve in March 2000 and March 2003. In 2000, 1-year rates were around 6.4% dropping to long-term yields of 4.5%. Three years later long rates were about the same but short rates were at about 3.5%.

In addition, there are a wide range of other behaviours shown by yield curves, described variously as monotonic, humped and S-shaped. Figure 4.3 shows the same market with humped curves, where highest rates are reached in the 5 to 10-year maturity period, but rates drop off at the short and long end of the curve.

Lastly, we also come across cases where curves are almost flat. Figure 4.4 shows US Treasury actives in July 1998. There is very little difference between 1-year and 30-year yields.

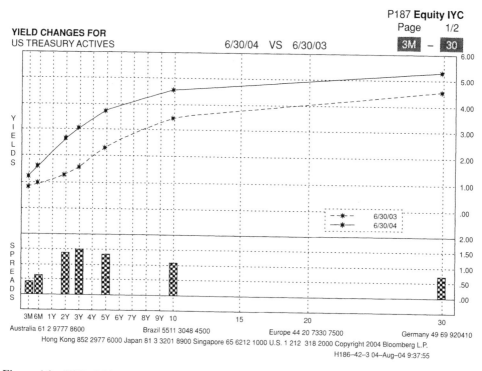

Figure 4.1 USD yield curves from June 2003 to June 2004
Used with permission from Bloomberg L.P.

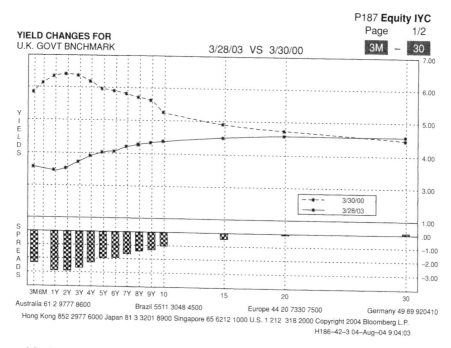

Figure 4.2 UKP yield curves from March 2000 to March 2003
Used with permission from Bloomberg L.P.

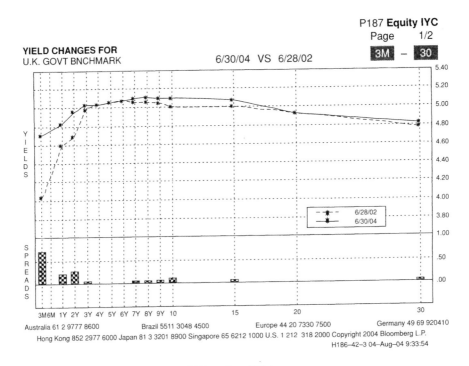

Figure 4.3 GBP yield curve from June 2002 to June 2004
Used with permission from Bloomberg L.P.

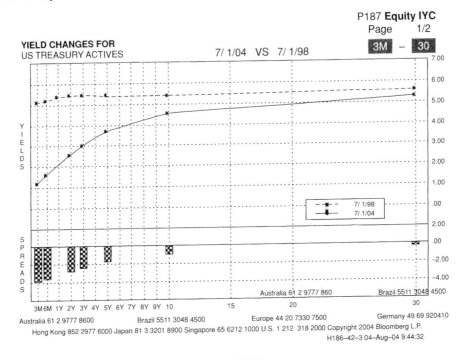

Figure 4.4 USD yield curve from July 1998 to July 2004
Used with permission from Bloomberg L.P.

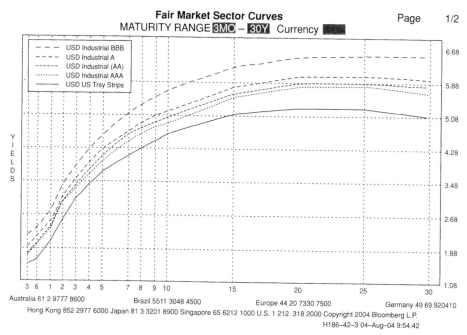

Figure 4.5 USD credit curves for US Treasury strips, USD AAA, AA, A, BBB industrials
Used with permission from Bloomberg L.P.

4.12 CREDIT CURVES

All the examples shown so far have come from the highest-rated bonds. In addition to these AAA issues, there exists a wide market in other instruments with lower credit ratings and hence higher yields (see Figure 4.5).

The difference between the reference yield curve and a lower-rated curve is called the *credit spread*. Typically, the credit spread will widen at times of economic recession, because the perceived risks of investing in corporate or other lower-rated bonds are higher.

4.13 FINDING YIELD CURVE DATA

Yield curve data is widely available from a range of sources. For instance, the *Financial Times* publishes gilt data, and a range of yield curve information is available from Bloomberg pages IYC, CURV, and YCRV.

5
Interest Rate Risk and Portfolio Management

5.1 INTRODUCTION

This chapter describes some of the basic concepts of fixed income risk management. In particular, we show ways in which portfolio managers take risk, or hedge it away, and some of the mathematical and graphical tools used for this purpose.

5.2 RETURN IN FIXED INCOME PORTFOLIOS

The first source of return in a fixed income portfolio is movements in the various yield curves that drive the pricing and returns of the securities in the portfolio and benchmark. For this reason, we give a brief introduction to commonly used interest rate sensitivity measures, and show how simplistic descriptions of risk are not always appropriate for a complex fixed income portfolio.

The second source of return is the allocation of assets in the portfolio across the term structure.[1] This allocation is within the manager's control, subject to investment mandates and compliance requirements. Depending on the risk profile of the portfolio against its benchmark, identical yield curve movements can either generate profits or losses. The role of portfolio structure is described in the second part of this chapter.

5.3 RISK NUMBERS AND INTEREST RATE SENSITIVITY

The price of any fixed income security changes when its yield is changed. The amount by which a security's price changes with respect to changes in the underlying yield to maturity is approximated by a quantity called *modified duration*:[2]

$$MD = -\frac{1}{P}\frac{\partial P(y)}{\partial y}$$

so that

$$\delta P = -\frac{\partial P}{\partial y}\delta y = MD \cdot \delta y$$

Example: On 6th August 2004, a US Treasury bond with coupon of 4.25% and maturity of 15th August 2013 has a yield of 4.36%, a price of $101.205 per $100 face value, and a modified duration of 7.272 years.

---

[1] For instance, this means the proportion of the portfolio that has maturities lying between 0 and 1 years, the proportion with maturities between 1 and 2 years, etc.

[2] Also known as Fisher–Weil duration.

If the yield now rises to 4.40%, the price will fall by an amount

$$\delta P = -7.272 \times 0.04 = -0.291$$

so that the price becomes $101.205 - \$0.291 = \$100.914$, which is close to the true price of $100.911.

Other types of duration exist. For instance, a mortgage-backed security's price is sensitive to coupon spreads and volatility, and duration measures can be defined for these additional sources of risk.

In practice, deriving and using an algebraic expression for modified duration is a tedious procedure for all but the simplest securities. If one can calculate the market price of a security as a function of yield, it is often more convenient to use a numerical approximation:

$$MD = -\frac{P(y + \delta y) - P(y)}{\delta y \cdot P(y)}$$

where δy is a small number compared to y.

For a more accurate estimation of how the price of a security varies under a change in the yield, we can use a second-order expression for price sensitivity:

$$\delta P = \frac{\partial P}{\partial y} \delta y + \frac{1}{2} \frac{\partial^2 P}{\partial y^2} (\delta y)^2 \tag{5.1}$$

or

$$\delta P = -MD \cdot \delta y + \tfrac{1}{2} C (\delta y)^2$$

where

$$C = \frac{1}{P} \frac{\partial^2 P}{\partial y^2}$$

Here, C stands for *convexity*. As before, an algebraic expression describing convexity for most instruments is complex, and it is often convenient to calculate its value numerically as follows:

$$C = \frac{P(y + \delta y) - 2P(y) + P(y - \delta y)}{P(y)(\delta y)^2}$$

Fortunately, one seldom has to work out these quantities, since they are usually available from a range of sources.

Modified duration and convexity are collectively known as *risk numbers*.

5.4   AGGREGATING RISK NUMBERS

Given the duration and convexity of the instruments in a portfolio, the corresponding quantities for the portfolio as a whole are given by the expressions

$$MD = \frac{\sum_i EE_i \cdot MD_i}{\sum_i MV_i \cdot MD_i} \tag{5.2}$$

$$C = \frac{\sum_i EE_i \cdot C_i}{\sum_i MV_i \cdot C_i} \tag{5.3}$$

where:

MD_i is the modified duration of security i;
C_i is the convexity of security i;
MV_i is the market value of security i;
EE_i the effective exposure of security i.

(For securities such as bills and bonds, effective exposure is the same as market value. For futures, the market value can be zero but the effective exposure non-zero.)

5.5 HEDGING RISK

As described above, modified duration is a measurement of a portfolio's sensitivity to parallel movements in the yield curve. A simplistic way to hedge a portfolio's exposure to changes in interest rates is therefore to ensure that its modified duration is the same as its benchmark. This can be done by buying and selling various securities, including cash and futures, to ensure the risk numbers are equal.

This sort of hedging ignores the distribution of assets along the yield curve, and it is possible to form numerous portfolios with the same modified duration. For instance, a bond with a duration of 5 years has the same modified duration as a portfolio with half its assets in cash (which has zero duration, since its value is independent of changes in rates) and half in a bond with a duration of 10 years.

The next section will show that this can be a very poor way to hedge, since it does not take a portfolio's distribution along the yield curve into account.

5.6 PORTFOLIO STRUCTURE

Suppose we have a portfolio whose performance is being measured against a benchmark with 5 years modified duration, with an even distribution of assets along the yield curve. That is, 10% of the benchmark has 0–1 years maturity, 10% has 1–2 years maturity, and so on.

The portfolio's assets are clustered around the short and long ends of the term structure, but the overall modified duration and convexity are the same as the benchmark. If the curve moves up or down in a parallel manner, then the returns of both will be the same. This type of distribution is called a *barbell*.

The curve now steepens, so that long rates rise more than short rates. In this case, the price of assets at the long end of the curve will fall due to the inverse price–yield relationship for bonds. Since the portfolio has a larger proportion of its assets at the long end of the curve than the benchmark, its overall performance will be less than that of the benchmark, and the active return will be negative. In other words, the portfolio will have underperformed even though it was hedged against parallel yield curve movements.

Now, suppose the portfolio has a *bullet* structure, or one where the bonds in a portfolio are clustered about a single maturity. As before, the modified duration and convexity of the portfolio and benchmark are the same, but the portfolio's assets are clustered about the 5-year point.

In this case, a yield curve steepening will boost the portfolio's active return, since it has no assets in the poorly performing long maturities, while the benchmark does.

For a portfolio manager who takes anything more than a very simplistic view of future term structure movements, a knowledge of the structure of the portfolio against that of the

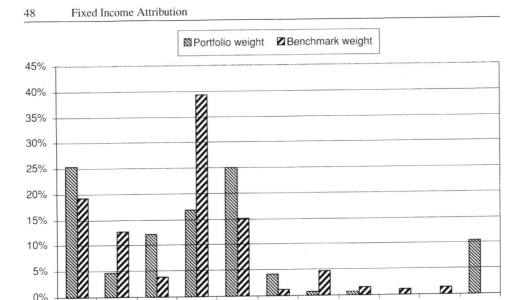

Figure 5.1 Sample maturity structure of portfolio against benchmark

benchmark is critical. This information is most easily conveyed in the form of a graph of market value exposures against maturity bucket (see Figure 5.1).

A graph of the difference in exposures between portfolio and benchmark is easier to read, and is informally known as a tombstone graph (see Figure 5.2). This example was taken from a real portfolio. As you can see, the risk profile is complex, and it is not easy to see how to hedge the portfolio against curve movements.

5.7 RISK IMMUNIZATION

A major part of a fund manager's mandate is to ensure that a fixed income portfolio is not exposed to unnecessary, or unintended, sources of risk.

Some risk simply cannot be hedged away. For instance, the only way to ensure that a portfolio will have exactly the same performance as its benchmark is to ensure that the portfolio has precisely the same set of cash flows as the benchmark. In practice, ensuring that relative market exposures are the same for portfolio and benchmark across (say) 1-year maturity buckets is probably enough to ensure term structure movement hedging – although this ignores credit spreads and other, non-term structure-related movements.

In practice, the situation is complicated by restrictions in asset classes that can be bought and sold to restructure a portfolio, including minimum deal sizes, the requirements of compliance mandates, and the optimization calculation. Finding a set of trades that match up the risk parameters and the exposure across maturity buckets can be a difficult problem, particularly when trade amounts are constrained to be multiples of a minimum trade lot size, and quite complex mathematical machinery can be required for a comprehensive solution.

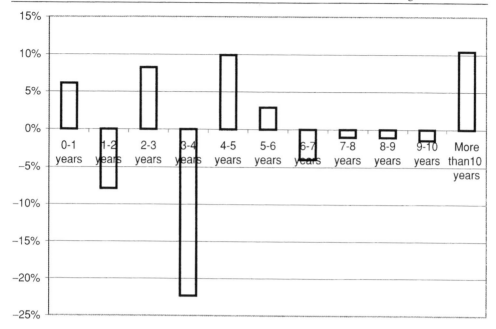

Figure 5.2   Relative maturity structure of portfolio against benchmark.

The situation is complicated still further when deliberate risks are to be taken. For instance, suppose the manager has a definite view that short-term rates will stay constant but that long-term rates will fall (a curve flattening). In this case, the best way to ensure that the portfolio will behave as expected may be to run a set of simulation calculations, showing how the performance of the portfolio and benchmark will vary under various curve movement types.

For instance, if a range of yield curve movements is imposed on the portfolio, and an attribution calculation run on these simulated returns shows that yield curve curvature returns are negligible, then the portfolio is probably hedged sufficiently against this type of risk.

Software systems are available to do exactly this. The current reference yield curve is displayed on the screen and the user can superimpose shift, twist and curvature movements. The portfolio and its benchmark have their performance calculated over a given number of days, with prices at the end of the interval calculated using the shifted curve. The user can run a number of pre-defined yield curve scenarios to see how well hedged the portfolio is against various types of curve movement.

Perhaps the hardest part of risk immunization is forming a proper idea of the risk/reward problems involved. What risks is the manager willing to take, and is it possible to measure these numerically? Inevitably the portfolio and its benchmark will respond to market movements in a variety of complex ways. A clear, definitive answer can only be given if the manager is able to assign expected probabilities to various yield curve movements, and then perform an analysis of the risk/reward tradeoffs for the performance results.

The analysis of attribution returns does not depend solely on movements in the yield curve, but also requires careful examination of the relationship between these movements and the structure of the portfolio. This requires close integration of the risk and return reporting systems. The implications of this requirement are considered further in Chapter 19.

6

Measuring Changes in Yield Curves

6.1 INTRODUCTION

Yield curves react continually to the current and future state of the economy, and a core task in fixed income asset management is to predict how the shape of curves will change. Only once this has been done can a managed portfolio be structured to take advantage of the expected movements.

In this chapter we discuss several techniques for describing and measuring changes in the shape of the curve, in ways that allow the user to relate the effects of these changes to investment decisions.

6.2 CURVE SHAPES

For the purposes of attribution analysis, it is normally possible to take the yield curve as a given. What is of more importance in performance analysis is to describe the *shape* of the curve in ways that allow its changes, and their effect on performance, to be measured.

For instance, if the user has made an investment decision that involves a parallel shift in the yield curve, then it is vital to be able to measure the parallel movement of the curve over the current interval, and to separate this movement from other types of curve movement. Separating these types of movement, and apportioning their effects on the security's overall performance, is the central topic of this chapter.

6.3 CURVES – THE RAW DATA

Yield curves are usually quoted at a range of different maturities. For instance, the Bloomberg fair value curve gives yields at 3 and 6 months, 1-, 2-, 3-, 5-, 7-, 10-, 15-, 20- and 30-year maturities. In this case, the change in a curve over a given period of time is therefore a set of 11 numbers:

$$\delta Y = (\delta y_1, \delta y_2, \delta y_3, \ldots, \delta y_{11}) \tag{6.1}$$

where

$$\delta y_i = Y_i^{T+1} - Y_i^T \tag{6.2}$$

We can stop here and say that this set of numbers encapsulates all the behaviour of the curve. However, it is not at all clear how this change vector may be linked to the investment decisions made by the manager.

6.4 A TYPICAL CURVE MOVEMENT

Firstly, what sort of yield curve movements occur?

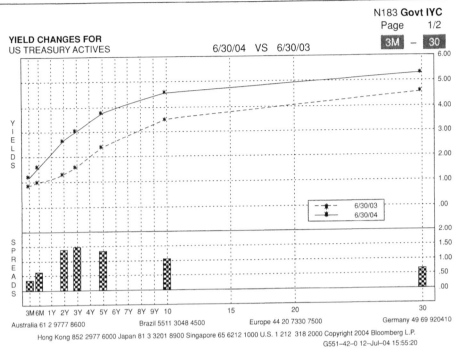

Figure 6.1   Change in yield curve for US Treasury actives from June 2003 to June 2004
Used with permission from Bloomberg L.P.

Figure 6.1 illustrates how a representative yield curve changed over a period of a year. Even with only seven data points, there are at least three types of change present:

1. Over the 12 months of activity shown, the yield curve as a whole has clearly moved upwards by an average of around 50 basis points. This is referred to as a *shift*, or parallel, motion.
2. The movement is not equal across all maturities. The movement at the short end of the curve is about 25 basis points upwards, while at the long end it is about 65 basis points. On this basis, we might say that the curve has become steeper – it shows more *twist*.
3. This steepening is not uniform. The spread increase over this 12-month period has been widest in the 2- to 3-year maturity region, where yields have increased by around 150 basis points. Alternatively, the curve has clearly become steeper at the short end of the curve than at the long end. In other words, the graph has become more *curved*, or has shown *butterfly* characteristics.[1]

   This is unfortunate for portfolios that are overweight the 2- to 3-year part of the curve, even if they have the same global duration as the benchmark. Such portfolios will underperform relative to the benchmark, even though they are hedged against parallel movements of the yield curve upwards or downwards.

The change in the shape of the curve is, of course, more complex than can be accounted for using these 'shift, twist, curvature' labels. In addition, the interpretation of points 2 and

---

[1] Presumably, this term arose because a graph showing simultaneous increase and decrease in curvature resembles the wings of a butterfly.

3 is entirely subjective. We could equally well argue that the curve is no more sloped than it was before, and that the change in shape is entirely due to a mixture of shift and curvature movements. Finding ways to describe such movements *unambiguously* is therefore an important area in attribution.

Fixed income attribution analysis should include all these effects in explaining how the distribution of a portfolio's assets across maturities generated over- or underperformance. As any practising manager will testify, identifying which source of risk generated profits or losses is not just an academic exercise. If an annual bonus is linked to how effectively a particular team carried out their job, then it is vital to be able to decide whether or not that job was done correctly.

6.5   DESCRIBING CURVE CHANGES

The most important part about interpreting curve changes is that the analysis should reflect the expectations of the user. If the manager's view is that the curve moved downwards across all maturities (that is, a shift motion only), but the attribution report shows substantial returns due to other effects, then the manager will be left puzzled and in doubt about the value of attribution analysis. It is therefore vitally important to choose an interpretation of shift, twist and butterfly that matches the user's view of curve movements.

Unfortunately, shift, twist and butterfly are actually rather vaguely defined terms that can be interpreted in several different ways, and they should accordingly be used with a great deal of care. For instance, consider a yield curve that moves up by 100 basis points at the short end, and up by 25 basis points at the long end, as shown in Figure 6.2.

At the most basic level, we can describe this curve change as a parallel movement, plus curve effects. The average movement is upwards by about 37 basis points, but this ignores the quite

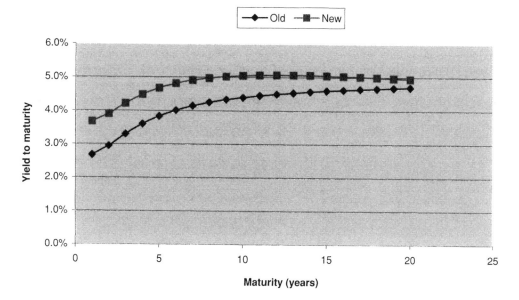

Figure 6.2   Sample yield curve graph, before and after a 100 basis point upwards movement at the short end and a 25 basis point upwards movement at the long end

substantial curve flattening. In fact, most of the curve movement comes from the flattening, so this description is rather misleading.

However, if we try to include shift and twist in the description of the curve change, the sizes of the movements are also unclear. Should we regard this curve change as:

- A parallel shift of +100 basis points, with a downwards movement of 75 basis points at the long end of the curve?
- A parallel shift of +25 basis points, with an upwards movement of 75 basis points at the short end of the curve?
- Something in between?

If we graph the parallel and twist movements, a simple geometrical solution suggests itself. This is to interpret the twist movement as a *rotation* around some twist point. Even if one averages curve movements to get the overall parallel shift, one has implicitly defined a twist point lying at the average maturity of yields making up the yield curve.

Is it possible to interpret curve movements independently of twist position? Unfortunately not, as the following example shows.

Suppose that, during a given month, a curve moves downwards by 50 basis points at the short end, while staying the same at the long end. The curve has steepened, but there is no parallel motion, so the attribution returns due to parallel shifts are zero. We might say the curve has twisted about the long end of the curve.

During the next month, the same curve subsequently moves downwards by 50 basis points at the long end, while staying the same at the short end. The curve has now flattened, again with no parallel motion, so again the attribution returns due to parallel shifts are zero. In this case, the curve has twisted about the short end of the curve.

However, the curve movement at the start and end of the 2-month interval is a parallel downwards movement of 50 basis points, which will generate non-zero returns for the parallel shift analysis. But the sum of the parallel returns calculated taking each month separately is zero.

As this example shows, *twist points must always be set at the outset*. One cannot pick and choose a twist point to suit a particular month's curve movements, as it is not possible to combine the attribution returns so calculated with attribution returns from previous months.

One solution might be to define a curve's parallel movement as the average change in the term structure across the entire interval, as previously. In this case, the curve shift would be 37 basis points. However, this is not an entirely satisfactory solution, because it presupposes that any curve twists are rotations about the mean maturity. It also means that returns at the short and long end of the curve will show the largest twist returns, which may be quite different to what the user expects.

This has major implications for the way that we describe attribution results. This simple example shows that we can only measure shift and twist movements unambiguously if we have pre-defined a curve twist point. If this curve twist point is chosen wrongly, the results of the attribution will show very large shift movements and equally large twist movements with the opposite sign, when the user may just be expecting a small shift movement.

An incorrect twist point may well result in the results of an attribution analysis differing from expectations. For instance, suppose that the twist point in the previous example is set at the long end of the curve. The first month will show zero parallel shift and a −50 basis point twist shift. However, the second month will show a −50 basis point parallel shift and a +50 basis point twist. This may require some explanation to a user who sees the second month's curve shift as a twist about the short end, since the results will be quite different to what was expected.

The moral is: use the terms shift, twist and butterfly with great caution! If a portfolio has made or lost a substantial part of its return from curve shifts, you must be clear about the role of the twist point when presenting the results of such an analysis. If the results do not agree with intuition, it may be preferable to show the returns in terms of a risk/attribution graph, as shown in Chapter 19.

6.5.1 Should one go any further?

It is, of course, grossly simplistic to expect three parameters to encapsulate all types of yield curve movement. A curve with 11 points needs a function with up to 11 separate arguments to describe it accurately.

The problem is that describing curve movements to this level of detail conveys little useful information to the user. There is therefore a point at which we should stop trying to describe curve movements, and accept that there will always be a small component of return that is not described by any of these effects. The market consensus appears to be that curve butterfly effects are about as far as one should go, since further detail is hard to interpret and is unlikely to form part of any investment process. I am certainly unaware of any fund managers who talk about gross curve movements at any deeper level.

It may, however, make sense for different managers to manage different parts of the curve. For instance, many fund managers have specialists to run the cash book, which consists of securities with short (< 1 year) maturities. These securities are priced off the bill curve, which may move in various ways that are unrelated to the overall yield curve. The cash book managers can then describe movements in their part of the curve in terms of short term shift, twist and butterfly, which may bear little relation to changes in the rest of the curve.

6.5.2 Can one use other movement descriptions?

One of the first papers on attribution used step functions to model curve changes (Kahn, 1991), while principal component analysis describes curve changes in terms of movement in various directions (Barber and Copper, 1996). Mathematically, these are both perfectly sound ways of breaking down curve changes into sub-components. The problem is that the sub-components often mean little more to the investor than did the initial raw data. It is therefore important to describe curve changes in terms that make sense to the manager who made the investment decisions, and for this reason we use the shift, twist and butterfly labels in much of what follows.

Other yield curve models have used polynomial splines, exponential splines, and B-splines (Anderson *et al.*, 1996). However, these models are not particularly suitable for attribution analysis as they cannot represent the global shape of a yield curve in terms of a small number of parameters.

6.6 WORKED EXAMPLES

In the remaining sections we outline several ways of describing changes, at various levels of detail. We will decompose the returns into shift, twist and butterfly components, but the user should note the caveats mentioned above. The techniques will be illustrated with Euro par curve data from Bloomberg; see Table 6.1 and Figure 6.3.

Table 6.1 Sample yield curve constituents, times to maturity and par yields

ISIN code	Maturity	TTM: 31-Dec-2003	Par yield on 31-Dec-2003 (%)	Par yield on 31-Jan-2004 (%)
DE0001137040	16-Dec-05	1.9616	2.591	2.510
DE0001141380	18-Aug-06	2.6329	2.851	2.721
DE0001141406	17-Aug-07	3.6301	3.223	3.104
DE0001141430	10-Oct-08	4.7808	3.498	3.396
DE0001135135	4-Jan-11	7.0164	3.767	3.680
DE0001135168	4-Jan-11	7.0164	3.953	3.875
DE0001135192	4-Jan-12	8.0164	4.101	4.036
DE0001135218	4-Jan-13	9.0192	4.206	4.145
DE0001135242	4-Jan-14	10.0192	4.286	4.236
FR0000189151	25-Apr-19	15.3260	4.664	4.660
DE0001134922	4-Jan-24	20.0247	4.812	4.807
DE0001135226	4-Jul-34	30.5288	4.937	4.932

Source: Bloomberg.

6.7 MODEL-FREE REPRESENTATIONS OF CURVES

In this case, no smoothing or modelling is performed on the raw yield curve data. For each instrument, the change of yield due to the Treasury curve is calculated by reading off an interpolated yield from the raw curve data, using the current security's maturity or duration.

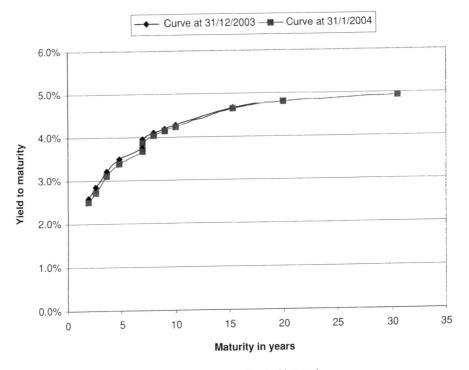

Figure 6.3 Graphs of sample yield curves at start and end of interval
Source: Bloomberg.

Simple linear or cubic interpolation is suitable (Press *et al.*, 1992). In this case, the only assumption we need make about the form of the yield curve is that it follows a simple function between sample points.

For instance, suppose we have an instrument with a maturity of 12 years. The closest points on the supplied yield curve have maturities of 10.0192 years and 15.3260 years, at which the curve has yields of 4.286% and 4.664%, respectively. The interpolated yield can then be calculated from

$$Y(x) = \frac{(x - x_1)}{(x_0 - x_1)} y_0 + \frac{(x - x_0)}{(x_1 - x_0)} y_1 \tag{6.3}$$

which in this example gives an interpolated yield of 4.427% at a maturity of 12 years.

Simple interpolation may be useful when the yield curve is particularly noisy or there are very few data points, and it is known that a multi-factor model will only roughly fit the observed market yields. In this case the attribution analysis may show large and unwarranted security-specific returns, which are simply an artefact of the fact that all curve yields lie some distance away from the smoothed values.

The great advantage of an unfitted curve mode is that it requires no assumptions about what sort of function represents the curve, apart from interpolation between grid points. In addition, there are no residuals (see below). The disadvantage is that it tells us nothing about the fine structure of the curve movements, but simply returns an amount for the movement of a curve as a whole at a given maturity, rather than breaking this movement down into sub-components. However, this may be exactly what is required. For instance, in measuring spread returns between, say, the BBB and CCC curves, all one usually requires is the total yield change component.

This representation does not decompose curve movements down into sub-components, so the warnings about the interpretation of shift, twist and butterfly do not apply.

To fit curve data in this way requires access to the raw curve data, which may have an impact on the data flow of the system.

6.8   FITTED MODEL REPRESENTATIONS

The rest of the yield curve descriptions in this chapter involve fitting some sort of model to the curve at the start and end of the interval, and then viewing changes in the curve in terms of changes to the model's parameters. The candidates are in the form of mathematical functions defined in terms of a small number of parameters.

While this approach allows a much deeper analysis of the yield curve's movements, it has the disadvantage that any model with a reasonable number of parameters is unlikely to fit the curve data exactly. The result is that when using a model fit to a curve, there will always be a *residual* component of yield change that cannot be accounted for in terms of movements in the fitted curves. Naturally, the better the model fit to the curve, the smaller the residual yield.

6.9   SHIFT AND CURVE POSITIONING ANALYSIS

The most common fixed-income risk decision type is to set one of the portfolio's duration measures against its benchmark. As discussed in the previous chapter, modified duration is a measure of the price sensitivity of the portfolio to parallel shifts in the underlying yield curve. This type of positioning is simply a bet that the curve will move up, or down, in a parallel manner.

The first yield curve statistic to measure is therefore its parallel shift upwards or downwards. This is perfectly straightforward to calculate; it can simply be taken as the arithmetic average of the changes in yield:

$$\delta y_{\text{shift}} = \frac{\sum_i \delta y_i}{n} \tag{6.4}$$

The amount of shift can be affected by a large number of data points towards the short end of the curve, so a weighting scheme that gives equal influence to yields at all parts of the curve may be preferable in practice.

Some managers stop here. For multi-currency bond portfolios, much of the risk is taken in the form of country bets, or allocation across different currencies, followed by duration bets on individual yield curves. Further bets on the shape of the yield curve are not taken, because it is simply too difficult and time-consuming to restructure individual portfolios when several thousand assets are held. In this case, the remaining yield shift is called curve shift and is measured as the difference between the overall security shifts and the parallel shift (which is the same for all securities):

$$\delta y_{\text{curve}} = \delta y - \delta y_{\text{shift}} \tag{6.5}$$

This curve shift includes all twist, butterfly, credit and other effects; it is a catch-all term for non-duration returns.

6.10   POLYNOMIAL TERM STRUCTURE MODELS

For polynomial modelling, we fit an expression of the form

$$y(m) = a_0 + a_1 m + a_2 m^2 \tag{6.6}$$

to the yield curve. This is a straightforward second-order polynomial, familiar from high-school mathematics classes. Depending on the values of a_0, a_1 and a_2, this expression can model a straight line, a slanted line or a parabola. If the curve changes shape, the values of the coefficients will vary over time.

A twist point can be added to this expression by rescaling the independent variable m by an amount S, so that

$$y(m) = a_0 + a_1(m - S) + a_2(m - S)^2 \tag{6.7}$$

With this modification, a curve rotation about maturity S will be expressed entirely as twist without any parallel movement.

Yield contributions from shift, twist and butterfly curve movements may then be calculated as follows:[2]

$$\delta y_{\text{shift}} = a_0^{t+1} - a_0^t \tag{6.8}$$

$$\delta y_{\text{twist}} = \left(a_1^{t+1} - a_1^t\right) \cdot (m - S) \tag{6.9}$$

$$\delta y_{\text{butterfly}} = \left(a_2^{t+1} - a_2^t\right) \cdot (m - S)^2 \tag{6.10}$$

The great advantage of a polynomial representation is that it is straightforward to identify the meaning of the various terms. The disadvantages are as follows:

---

[2] Note that any change in maturity over the calculation interval is not included in these expressions, implying that roll return must be calculated separately. See Chapter 11 for more information about the relationship between curve changes and roll return.

- The curve is not well behaved at the long end, since the yield rises as the square of the maturity. The yield does not therefore tend to a constant value at high maturities.
- Even if two curves are quite similar at nearby dates, the polynomial coefficients can differ widely between the two, and this can give rise to spurious attribution returns.

6.10.1 Example 1: Worked example for polynomial model

A worked example with different twist points is instructive. Fitting expression (6.7) to the raw data in Table 6.1, with values of $S = 0$ and $S = 30$, gives the sets of coefficients in Tables 6.2 and 6.3.

Now consider two securities with maturities of 1 and 30 years. Using expressions (6.8), (6.9) and (6.10) to give the shift, twist and butterfly components at a maturity of 1 and 30 years, we have for the case $S = 0$ the results in Table 6.4 and for the case $S = 30$ the results in Table 6.5. Although the effects add up to the same total result, the decomposition of yield changes is completely different.

For the case where the rotation point was at the short end of the curve, the movement at short maturities is entirely attributed to a curve shift. Even though the movement at the long end of the curve is virtually zero, it is still shown as a sum of large, non-zero curve movements.

Setting the rotation point to the long end of the curve gives results that are much more in keeping with expectations. At the short end of the curve, the curve shift is nearly zero and the

Table 6.2 Sample polynomial coefficients for twist point at $S = 0$, using data from Table 6.1

$S = 0$	31-Dec-03	31-Jan-04
a_0	2.387424	2.244824
a_1	0.234707	0.245975
a_2	−0.005063	−0.005281

Table 6.3 Sample polynomial coefficients for twist point at $S = 30$, using data from Table 6.1

$S = 30$	31-Dec-03	31-Jan-04
a_0	4.87231	4.871289389
a_1	−0.069069	−0.070896153
a_2	−0.005063	−0.00528168

Table 6.4 Shift, twist and butterfly returns for sample security with twist point at $S = 0$

$S = 0$	Maturity $= 1$	Maturity $= 30$
Shift	−0.143	−0.143
Twist	0.011	0.338
Butterfly	0.000	−0.196
TOTAL	−0.132	−0.001

Table 6.5   Shift, twist and butterfly returns for sample security
with twist point at $S = 30$

$S = 30$	Maturity $= 1$	Maturity $= 30$
Shift	−0.001	−0.001
Twist	0.053	0.000
Butterfly	−0.184	0.000
TOTAL	−0.132	−0.001

yield movement is attributed to a combination of curve flattening and lessening in curvature.
At the long end of the curve, nothing much has changed.

In terms of producing comprehensible results, the placement of the twist point is therefore
crucial.

6.11   NELSON–SIEGEL TERM STRUCTURE MODELS

An alternative approach uses the Nelson–Siegel formulation to model benchmark and credit
curves. From their 1987 paper (Nelson and Siegel, 1987), a good fit to a set of market forward
rates is usually given by

$$r(m) = \beta_0 + \beta_1 \exp\left(-\frac{m}{\tau}\right) + \beta_2\left[\left(\frac{m}{\tau}\right)\exp\left(\frac{m}{\tau}\right)\right] \tag{6.11}$$

where $r(m)$ is the market forward rate for maturity m, and $\beta_0, \beta_1, \beta_2$ are parameters that are
varied to fit the shape of the underlying curve, while τ is a scale length factor.

Market yields $R(m)$ are then calculated from

$$R(m) = \frac{1}{m}\int_0^m r(\tau)\mathrm{d}\tau \tag{6.12}$$

which gives

$$R(m) = \beta_0 + (\beta_1 + \beta_2)\frac{\left[1 - \exp\left(-\frac{m}{\tau}\right)\right]}{\left(\frac{m}{\tau}\right)} - \beta_2 \exp\left(-\frac{m}{\tau}\right) \tag{6.13}$$

This has the convenient feature that

$$R(m) \rightarrow (\beta_0 + \beta_1) \text{ as } m \rightarrow 0$$

and

$$R(m) \rightarrow \beta_0 \text{ as } m \rightarrow \infty$$

(i.e. the curve becomes asymptotically flat as m becomes large).

The family of curves generated by these functions behaves very much like real yield curves
as shown in Figure 6.4. A Nelson–Siegel function (as we shall call Equation (6.13)) is therefore
a good choice to use for attribution analysis.

Given a starting value of τ, Equation (6.13) is linear in $\beta_0, \beta_1, \beta_2$, which allows standard
curve-fitting techniques to be used to find values of the β coefficients (see Appendix A). Since
we are interested in the variation of these coefficients over time, it is necessary for τ to be fixed

Values of Nelson-Siegel function for various values of beta

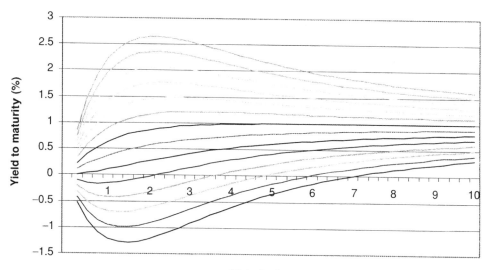

Maturity in years

Figure 6.4 Effects of varying β on the expression $R(m) = 1 - (1 - \beta) \cdot \left(\frac{1 - \exp(-m)}{m} - \beta \exp(-m)\right)$ where β lies between ± 6. For a non-inverted yield curve, β lies in the range $(-1$ to $1)$.
Source: After Nelson and Siegel (1987).

at the outset so that changes in its value cannot affect the curve shape. Nelson and Siegel note that there is a tradeoff in choosing a suitable value:

> Small values of τ correspond [to] rapid decay in the regressor and therefore will be able to fit curvature at low maturities well while being unable to fit excessive curvature over longer maturity ranges. Correspondingly, large values of τ produce slow decay in the regressors that can fit curvature over longer maturity ranges, but they will be unable to follow extreme curvature at short maturities.

The precise value chosen will depend on the characteristics of the yield curve under consideration. Based on our own research and some worked examples, a value for τ of around 30% of the highest maturity appears to be a suitable starting point.

Since the form of this equation is unchanged under a change in variable

$$\frac{m}{\tau} \to m'$$

no information is lost if we set τ to 1 and move any maturity rescaling into the raw data, so that Equation (6.13) reads

$$R(m) = \beta_0 + (\beta_1 + \beta_2)\frac{[1 - \exp(-m)]}{m} - \beta_2 \exp(-m) \tag{6.14}$$

Throughout the remainder of the book, τ therefore does not appear in the worked examples.

More complex expressions based on the Nelson–Siegel function can form an even better fit to real-world yield curve data. A paper from the Royal Bank of Canada describes a five-parameter Nelson–Siegel model (Bolder and Streliski, 1999) as well as several other sophisticated approaches to yield curve modelling.

To include a curve twist point, we again introduce a maturity scale length, S, which may be interpreted as the maturity about which a yield curve twist is occurring. Then we can set

$$R_0(m) = \beta_0 + \beta_1 \exp(-S) \tag{6.15}$$

$$R_1(m) = \beta_1 \left[\frac{1 - \exp(-t)}{t} - \exp(-S) \right] \tag{6.16}$$

$$R_2(t) = \beta_2 \left[\frac{1 - \exp(-t)}{t} - \exp(-t) \right] \tag{6.17}$$

where R_0, $R_0 + R_1$, $R_0 + R_1 + R_2$ are successively closer fits to Equation (6.13). In the case of $S = 0$, R_0 reduces to $\beta_0 + \beta_1$ (the asymptotic yield as $m \to 0$) and we interpret the shift movement as a twist about zero maturity. In the case that $S \to \infty$, R_0 reduces to β_0 (the asymptotic yield as $m \to \infty$) and we interpret the shift movement as a twist about long-term maturity. Twists about other maturities are calculated by setting S appropriately. Note that R_2 is independent of S, since in the Nelson–Siegel formulation the amount of curvature is purely a function of m and β_2, and is not subject to the same indeterminacy as yield curve twists.

Yield contributions from shift, twist and butterfly curve movements may then be calculated as follows:

$$\delta y_{\text{shift}} = \left[\beta_0^{t+1} + \beta_1^{t+1} \exp(-S) \right] - \left[\beta_0^t + \beta_1^t \exp(-S) \right] \tag{6.18}$$

$$\delta y_{\text{twist}} = \left(\beta_1^{t+1} - \beta_1^t \right) \left[\frac{1 - \exp(-m)}{m} - \exp(-S) \right] \tag{6.19}$$

$$\delta y_{\text{butterfly}} = \left(\beta_2^{t+1} - \beta_2^t \right) \left[\frac{1 - \exp(-m)}{m} - \exp(-m) \right] \tag{6.20}$$

6.11.1   Example 2: Worked example for Nelson–Siegel model

Based on the same raw data used in Example 1, and using an illustrative value of $\tau = 1$, the two yield curves are described by the values in Table 6.6.

Using Equations (6.18), (6.19) and (6.20), we have for the case $S = 0$ the results in Table 6.7 and for the case $S = 30$ the results in Table 6.8.

Table 6.6   Sample Nelson–Siegel coefficients

$T = 0$	31-Dec-03	31-Jan-04
β_0	5.169176	5.194717
β_1	−0.026900	0.718639
β_2	−8.453695	−9.916285

Table 6.7   Shift, twist and butterfly returns for sample security with $T = 0$

$T = 0$	Maturity $= 1$	Maturity $= 30$
Shift	29.98%	29.98%
Twist	19.70%	−24.94%
Butterfly	−38.65%	−4.88%
TOTAL	11.03%	0.16%

Table 6.8   Shift, twist and butterfly returns for sample security with twist point at $T = 30$

$T = 30$	Maturity = 1	Maturity = 30
Shift	2.55%	2.55%
Twist	47.13%	2.49%
Butterfly	−38.65%	−4.88%
TOTAL	11.03%	0.16%

The results are very similar to those in the polynomial model. Depending on where the shift point is placed, results are either intuitive ($S = 30$) or counter-intuitive ($S = 0$).

6.12   PRINCIPAL COMPONENT ANALYSIS

The simplest type of fixed income interest rate hedge assumes that term structures only move in a parallel manner. So far we have described these motions by fitting mathematical models to the shape of the term structure at the start and end of the interval, and monitored how the parameters for this model have varied.

A more realistic description acknowledges that the term structure moves in a more complex manner with (perhaps) more degrees of freedom than can be modelled using the functions introduced. Principal component analysis is a very general approach that describes changes in the shape of the yield curve in terms of movements in several directions.

Suppose that the change in the yield curve is described by a set of yield changes at given maturities:

$$\delta Y = (\delta y_1, \delta y_2, \delta y_3, \ldots, \delta y_n) \tag{6.21}$$

The idea behind principal component analysis is that this vector can be written as a sum of other vectors:

$$\delta Y = \sum_{i=1}^{n} w_k X_k \tag{6.22}$$

where the vectors X_k are orthonormal. Each orthonormal vector describes a direction in which the curve can move.

Some authors have suggested that a portfolio can be immunized against yield curve shifts by immunizing against movements in each direction. For such an approach to work, the types and directions of such movements should be consistent across time. Barber and Copper (1996) identify 10 fundamental directions in which the curve shifts within their sample data set.

For attribution purposes, one would use a principal component decomposition for analysis of returns if that was the way the portfolio's risk had been hedged. Instead of describing performance in terms of return generated by shift, twist, etc., one would describe it in terms of movement type 1, movement type 2, and so on. The sum of each movement at each maturity would add up to the actual yield movement for that maturity.

If a portfolio has been hedged using the results of a principal component analysis, then it makes sense to produce an attribution analysis based on the same breakdown of curve movements. For presentation of results, however, the utility of this approach is not so clear, particularly in cases where the individual curve movements do not have a straightforward interpretation.

6.13   FITTING DATA TO MODELS

The coefficients in Tables 6.2, 6.3 and 6.6 may be calculated using a standard technique, called a least squares fit. This involves construction of the normal equations, which is covered in Appendix A.

6.14   CONSTRAINTS IN CURVE FITTING

There are two important constraints to observe when fitting curves to data:

• curves that should not overlap, do not do so;
• interest rates cannot become negative.

If these constraints need to be incorporated into the least squares fit, the problem becomes substantially more complex and a different approach may be in order. In this case either the source of the raw data, or the necessity of using small numbers of noisy yields, should be reconsidered.

7
Converting Yield Movements
into Performance

Unlike equities, the price – and hence the return – of a fixed income instrument depends on a wide range of market inputs. Foremost amongst these is the security's *yield*. Given the current yield to maturity of a security (or more generally, the yield curve) we can price all future cash flows for the security, add them together, and work out the price of the security at various dates together with its cash flows. From this information, we can work out performance.

The previous chapters have considered how yield changes in response to various sources of risk, and how a security's yield change can be decomposed into yield changes from Treasury curve risk, credit spreads, and other effects. The next step in an attribution analysis is to examine, in detail, how to translate these movements in yield into performance contributions.

In this chapter, we discuss how the effect of a yield change affects the return of a security, and outline practical ways of calculating the return. This is the point at which changes in yield curves impact on portfolio performance, so this is a central topic in accurate fixed income attribution.

For example, we know that a yield curve has moved upwards by 10 basis points. How has this affected the performance of a bond? To do this, we need to work out how the price of a security changes when its yield changes. There are two approaches:

(i) reprice the security from first principles, or
(ii) use a perturbational approach.

7.1 PRICING FROM FIRST PRINCIPLES

The first-principles approach requires the capability to price the security from information such as maturity, coupon and valuation of cash flows. The mechanics of pricing a bond from its constituent cash flows are so widely known that we will not cover the subject here.

In fact, the majority of government bonds are more conveniently priced using standard formulae. For instance, the price of an Australian government bond is given by

$$P = v^{f/d} \left[g(c - a_{\overline{n}}) + 100v^n \right] \tag{7.1}$$

where:

P is the price per \$100 face value;
$v = \frac{1}{1+i}$ where $100i$ is the half-yearly yield to maturity (%);
f is the number of days from the settlement date to the next coupon payment date;
d is the number of days in the current coupon period;
g is half the annual coupon rate;
n is the number of coupon payment periods from the next coupon payment to maturity;
$a_{\overline{n}} = \frac{1-v^n}{i}$;
c is 0 if the bond is ex-interest, and 1 otherwise.

There are various additional conventions to apply if the bond is in the final coupon period, in which case it is priced as a bill.

In practice every bond type has its own pricing conventions regarding settlement periods, ex-interest periods, calculation of accrued interest and day-counts, and treatment of non-standard first and last periods. A useful reference is 'Government Bond Outlines' (J.P. Morgan, 2001).

The use of a pricing formula gives almost identical results to pricing from first principles. The difference in price arises from the assumption that coupons are not discounted at the current yield to maturity. In practice, the price given by the formula is taken as definitive.

7.2 MEASURING THE EFFECTS OF YIELD CURVE SHIFTS

Initially, the security has a market yield y_0 at time t_0. Substituting this yield and the relevant settlement date into the pricing formula gives the security price, P_0.

Suppose we now measure the effect of the change in yield due to the parallel yield shift, which you have previously worked out. This will give the price of the security P_1 with the yield changed by this effect only. That is, the price so calculated only includes parallel yield curve shift. The change in price $P_1 - P_0$, divided by the initial price P_0, is the return due to parallel yield shift.

Repeat this process with all other sources of yield change, until all effects have been included and we are using the actual market yield at time t_1. The sum of the partial returns will be the actual market return for the security.

This is a simple to understand, transparent way to translate yield changes into performance changes. Unfortunately, it is also one that requires a great deal of effort. The main objection is not theoretical but practical; it assumes we can actually price the securities in our portfolios.

For relatively simple instruments such as bank bills and government bonds, this is not too much of a hardship; these need only be set up once and then simply require a daily yield to be repriced correctly. Pricing libraries are commercially available for the majority of such instruments, or you can write a library yourself.

However, matters are more complex for other classes of instrument, such as floating rate notes, swaps and OTC derivatives. For instance, an FRN that has a monthly update period needs its coupon to be updated 12 times during the year in order to price correctly. Matters become still more difficult for complex derivatives and large benchmarks, or for portfolios with many hundreds of FRNs. Very quickly, the data maintenance requirements become unsustainable.

A second issue is that if we are basing our attribution analysis on internally calculated prices, it is vital to check that the prices and returns so calculated actually match up with the returns from the back office. In effect, we are running two parallel performance measurement systems. This means reconciliation reports, someone to look at the reports, and an audit process to track down any discrepancies. While having an independent check on the accuracy of the back office's returns may be useful, it is probably not what you expected to have to do when setting up an attribution system.

Thirdly, what happens when we introduce an instrument into the portfolio that we cannot price? For instance, some mortgage-backed securities require complex techniques to value that require many hours of computer time. Repricing such securities with a group of different yields is impractical.

Fourthly, if you are working on a per-security basis, can you reproduce benchmarks on this basis? Fixed income benchmarks can contain thousands of bonds from many different countries, each of which has to be accurately repriced every day in order to replicate the performance of the benchmark. The pricing assumptions underlying securities in many benchmarks are not always clear, or even documented, and it is often impractical to track down the source of every pricing discrepancy.

None of these considerations need be a problem if you are running attribution as part of an independent front-office risk and performance monitoring system. In this case, you will accept these data maintenance costs as part of the overhead of your system.

For managers who just want to run attribution, however, the overheads introduced by the individual security pricing approach are completely unacceptable. Very quickly, you will find you need to carry out:

- daily performance and pricing reconciliation;
- security maintenance;
- benchmark maintenance;
- variable coupon updates;
- cash flows entry;
- cash deposits and withdrawals;
- back-dated trades maintenance.

In other words, you will need personnel and data maintenance procedures to rival that of a typical back office, with all the costs this will bring.

Fortunately, there exists a viable and practical alternative.

7.3   PERTURBATIONAL PRICING

Let's go back to first principles and look at what drives the performance of a security. Instead of using prices and cash flows, an alternative way to calculate return is to use the expression

$$r = y \cdot \delta t - \text{MD} \cdot \delta y + \tfrac{1}{2}C(\delta y)^2 \qquad (7.2)$$

where:

r is the return of the security over the current interval;
y is the yield to maturity of the security;
δt is the interval (in years) over which the performance calculation is run;
MD is the modified duration of the security;
C is the convexity of the security;
δy is the change in the security's yield over the interval,

and

$$\delta y = |y_{T+1} - y_T| << 1 \qquad (7.3)$$

This breaks up the return of a security over an interval into three parts. If you are planning any serious work in fixed income attribution, it's worth writing this equation up on your whiteboard for reference, as it is used in much of the following text.

The $y \cdot \delta t$ term measures how much of the return is due to the security's yield to maturity. Even if the security yield change is zero over the given interval, this term implies that a bond paying a coupon will still show a positive return, since such an instrument accrues value over time due to coupon.

The $-\text{MD} \cdot \delta y$ term uses the modified duration of the security. This risk term gives a measure of how sensitive the security's price is to changes in yield. For instance, a bond might have a modified duration of 5 years. This means that for every basis point the security's yield rises, the price of the bond falls by $0.0001 \times 5 = 0.0005\%$. The negative sign shows that as yields fall, market prices rise, and vice versa.

Lastly, the $\frac{1}{2}C(\delta y)^2$ term uses the security's convexity to include second-order returns. This allows more accurate approximation to return than just using modified duration, which only captures first-order yield dependency.

Why is equation (7.2) useful? The reason is that, as long as we have values for a security's yield, modified duration and convexity, we can break down the performance of any security by source of risk, without needing any pricing tools. Moreover, it does not require that we calculate the price of a security before undertaking attribution.[1]

Are there any problems with this approach?

- δy is assumed to be small. This is usually the case for the fixed interest markets.
- Perturbational pricing is not as accurate as pricing from first principles. This is probably not a serious problem, in view of other sweeping assumptions that have to be made when quantifying yield curve movements.
- The approach requires that we have values for the security yield, modified duration and convexity. These quantities are widely available for virtually all liquid fixed income instruments, and may usually be downloaded from the same sources as pricing information.

In the author's opinion, the advantages of perturbational pricing far outweigh these minor problems.

- No pricing machinery, or knowledge about how the security is priced, is needed.
- No set-up data is required. The attribution system can sit on top of an existing performance calculation system.
- Portfolio sectors can be handled just as easily as single instruments (see Chapter 18 on benchmarks for more on why this matters).
- The technique is extremely fast. The calculations are simple enough to be handled within a database's stored procedures and may be coded in Transact-SQL (Kline *et al.*, 1999). This removes the necessity of retrieving large volumes of pricing data from a server, sending them to a client workstation, processing, and then returning the results to the server or the reporting tool. In turn the attribution engine reduces network loading, is much simpler to program, and allows economies of scale for data processing.

---

[1] This approach can be simplified still further. If we are willing to omit convexity return and roll several other small terms togther, we can run a simplified calculation without using modified duration and convexity at all. All that is needed is the security yield and a set of parameterized market yield curves.

Suppose we have return on a given security as r. Subtract the return due to yield, $y.\delta r$, to get return due to interest rate risk. Then all remaining return is due to the $-\text{MD}.\delta y$ term in Equation (7.2), and this can be decomposed on a *pro rata* basis.

This is definitely a lightweight approach to attribution, but it may be useful in some contexts:

$$r_{\text{shift}} = (r - y \cdot \delta t)\frac{\delta y_{\text{shift}}}{\delta y}$$

This approach spreads any residual return into the $-\text{MD}.\delta y$ term, so it is not quite as accurate as the full analysis.

Which attribution approach you use depends on how your existing system works. If it just imports prices and deal considerations without any pricing machinery, then you are probably constrained to using the perturbational approach. If you have the resources to price everything from first principles, you may still want to use the perturbational approach; it is relatively future-proof in that introducing new instrument types will not require major amounts of coding – and there will always be new instrument types; this is a fact of life in performance measurement.

Part II

Sources of Attribution Return

8
The Hierarchy of Fixed Income Returns

Part II of this book presents detailed descriptions of each of the sources of return available to a fixed income portfolio. Each source of return fits into a hierarchy, as shown in Figure 8.1.[1]

Depending on what set of attribution assumptions is used, this attribution tree will take on different forms. For instance, yield return can be left as is, or may be decomposed into subreturns. Each chapter in this section will display the relevant portions of this chart, adjusted to suit the current return decomposition.

For completeness, we have included currency returns in Figure 8.1, although these are not discussed in the current text.

8.1 SUBJECTIVITY IN ATTRIBUTION

There are many different types of decision that can be made when running a fixed interest portfolio, and many ways of interpreting the results. Part II of this book describes some of the attribution approaches that are currently used.

This means that, inevitably, there is some subjectivity in the analysis of fixed interest attribution returns. This subjectivity does not lie in the breakdown of the returns, which is a well-defined process once the attribution methodology has been agreed upon. Rather, the subjectivity comes from deciding on which attribution process to use. The types of decision are:

- which yield curve parameterization to use, and how to model movements in the yield curve;
- correlation of credit curve movements;
- whether to use a duration-based approach, or a yield curve-based approach;
- and many others.

For this reason, the author does not expect to see any standards for fixed income attribution appear in the near future, even if such standards become widespread for equity portfolios.

8.2 EXCESS PRECISION

A fact of life in carrying out fixed interest attribution is that there is no exact decomposition of returns by risk sectors, particularly where subjective yield curve fits are used. For instance, the choice between a polynomial and a Nelson–Siegel curve representation could easily result in the shift movement for a given instrument differing by tens of basis points. Neither number is wrong. The difference has arisen because of differing underlying assumptions about what representation is preferred, where the twist point occurs, which instruments are used to make up the yield curve, and so on.

---

[1] This diagram decomposes currency returns according to the Karnosky–Singer attribution model (Karnosky and Singer, 2000). Other equally valid decompositions are currency allocation and currency interaction components.

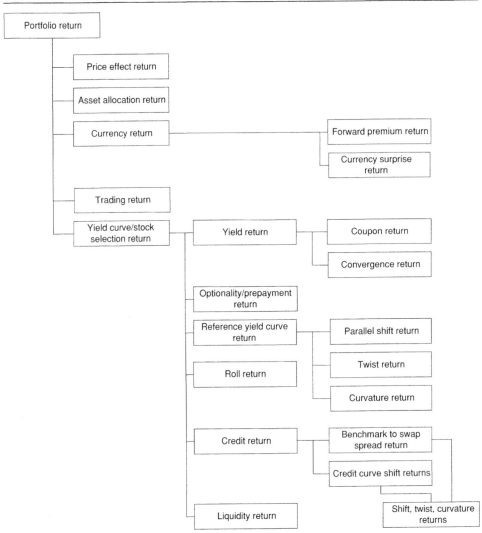

Figure 8.1 Sample attribution return hierarchy

In the face of these highly subjective assumptions that the user has to make, no accuracy is lost by using a simplified pricing approach for intermediate attribution calculations. Even when different attribution breakdowns are chosen, Spaulding's second law[2] of attribution returns – that the sum of the attribution returns must equal the excess return – is always obeyed.

---

[2] The three laws of attribution, as set out by Spaulding (2003b), are as follows.
First law: The attribution model should represent the active decisions of the portfolio manager.
Second law: The sum of the attribution returns must equal the excess return.
Third law: The sum of the linked attribution effects must equal the sum of the linked excess return.

9

Yield Return and Coupon Return

The first source of return in an attribution analysis is that due to the security's yield. Broadly speaking, this is the return shown by the security due to yield when nothing has changed in the marketplace except elapsed time. Roll return – which also assumes that market conditions do not change over time, and relies on the slope of the yield curve to enhance returns – is covered in Chapter 10.

Chapter 7 has shown that there are two ways to calculate such return: from first principles and from a perturbational approach. The two approaches do not give exactly comparable results, due to the different methodologies used. Whether this actually matters is a choice the user must make; our opinion is that it is unimportant.

9.1 YIELD RETURN

Yield return is also known as static return, carry return, or calendar return. Yield return measures the return of the security due to the passage of time. This is simply calculated as

$$r_{\text{yield}} = y_t \delta t \tag{9.1}$$

where y_t is the current yield to maturity of the security.

If required, this return may further be decomposed in two ways:

- coupon/convergence return;
- systematic/specific return.

9.2 DECOMPOSITION INTO COUPON AND CONVERGENCE RETURN

Yield return may be decomposed into the return from coupon payments, and return from the difference between the coupon and the security's yield. These returns are labelled as coupon return and convergence return, respectively:

$$r_{\text{yield}} = r_{\text{coupon}} + r_{\text{rolldown}} \tag{9.2}$$

See Figure 9.1.

9.3 COUPON RETURN

The coupon return is simply the product of coupon rate and time:

$$r_{\text{coupon}} = C \cdot \delta t \tag{9.3}$$

For a standard constant-coupon bond, this return is constant.

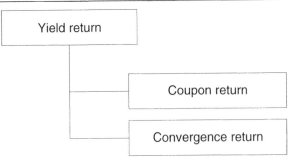

Figure 9.1   Decomposition of yield return into coupon return and convergence return

9.4 CONVERGENCE RETURN

Convergence return is calculated using the difference between the yield to maturity and the coupon rate, multiplied by elapsed time:

$$r_{\text{convergence}} = (y_t - C) \cdot \delta t \tag{9.4}$$

Often, the yield to maturity will differ substantially from the bond's coupon, depending on the current level of the yield curve and the security's time to maturity. However, as the bond approaches maturity the yield of the security will converge towards the coupon value. For this reason, this component of return is known as convergence return.

9.5 DECOMPOSITION INTO SYSTEMATIC AND SPECIFIC RETURN

In some circumstances it is useful to split the market yield to maturity of a security into the yield of a maturity-equivalent instrument on the sovereign curve, and a credit spread between this curve and the actual yield of the instrument. This allows the yield return to be viewed in terms of the return generated by high credit spreads. See Figure 9.2.

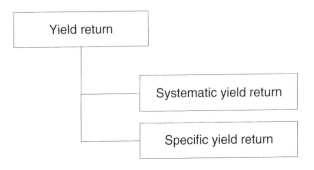

Figure 9.2   Decomposition of yield return into systematic/specific returns

9.6   CALCULATING YIELD RETURN

As will be apparent by now, yield return is not complex to calculate. Nevertheless, it can convey useful information about the make-up of a portfolio, such as the contribution made to performance by investing in high-yielding securities relative to the benchmark.

At the very least, this part of the attribution system should provide the following:

- A clear statement of how much return is due to yield effects, and how these yield effects are calculated.
- The ability to decompose yield returns into coupon returns and convergence returns.

10
Treasury Curve Return

10.1 MOVEMENTS IN THE TREASURY CURVE

Term structure return measures the return generated by movements in the Treasury curve for each market. Typically, movements in this curve are examined more closely than movements in credit curves because of its effect on the entire market.

The yield of all instruments will typically change over each interval. By examining how the Treasury curve moves, we can measure how much of each security's yield change is due to changes in the Treasury curve. Once we have this yield change, we can use the expression

$$r = -\text{MD} \cdot \delta y \tag{10.1}$$

to calculate the return generated. We consider three ways of examining Treasury curve movements.

10.2 NO CURVE ANALYSIS

In this case, no smoothing or modelling is performed on the raw yield curve data. For each instrument, the change of yield due to the Treasury curve is calculated by reading off an interpolated yield from the raw curve data, using the current security's maturity or duration.

This may be useful when the yield curve is particularly noisy, and it is known that a multi-factor model will only roughly fit the observed market yields. In this case the attribution analysis may show large and unwarranted security-specific returns, which arise because all curve yields lie some distance away from the smoothed values.

10.3 SHIFT/TWIST/BUTTERFLY

In this case, we form a model of the Treasury curve using a multi-factor model, and use this model to measure the contribution of various types of yield curve movement. As described in Chapter 6, some suitable models include second-order polynomials of the form

$$y(m) = a_0 + a_1 m + a_2 m^2 \tag{10.2}$$

and Nelson–Siegel functions

$$y(m) = a_0 + (a_1 + a_2)\frac{[1 - \exp(-m)]}{m} - a_2 \exp(-m) \tag{10.3}$$

or a simplified Nelson–Siegel function

$$y(m) = a_0 + a_1[1 - \exp(-m)] + a_2 t \exp(1 - t) \tag{10.4}$$

See Figure 10.1.

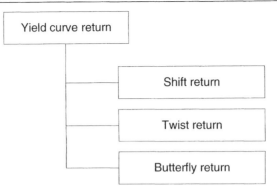

Figure 10.1   Decomposition of yield curve return into shift, twist and butterfly components

10.4   DURATION ATTRIBUTION

Duration attribution is a different way to look at term structure attribution. In essence, the benchmark return is calculated as if the benchmark has the portfolio's modified duration. This measures the effect the global duration bet had on the portfolio's excess return.

Duration attribution splits up yield curve movements in a different manner. Instead of the shift, twist, butterfly movement described above, we set yield curve movements to be the sum of duration returns and yield curve positioning returns.

Unlike the term structure attribution models described above, duration attribution requires a benchmark. Duration attribution returns include curve and credit effects, and the curve effect includes a duration return and a curve positioning effect.

Denote

$$r_{\text{yc}}^{\text{P}} = -\sum_{i=1}^{n} w_i^{\text{P}} \cdot \text{MD}_i^{\text{P}} \cdot \Delta y c_i \tag{10.5}$$

$$r_{\text{yc}}^{\text{B}} = -\sum_{i=1}^{m} w_i^{\text{B}} \cdot \text{MD}_i^{\text{B}} \cdot \Delta y c_i \tag{10.6}$$

where i ranges over a set of sectors. These two expressions represent the returns of a portfolio and a benchmark under a change in yield curve shape, where w_i is asset allocation, MD_i is modified duration, and $\Delta y c_i$ is the change in yield for sector i.

Then

$$\tilde{r}_{\text{yc}}^{\text{B}} = -\sum_{i=1}^{m} w_i^{\text{B}} \cdot \text{MD}_i^{\text{B}} \cdot \frac{\text{MD}_{\text{P}}}{\text{MD}_{\text{B}}} \Delta y c_i \tag{10.7}$$

represents the return of a nominal portfolio with weights equal to that of the benchmark, but modified duration equal to that of the portfolio.

$\Delta y c_i$ can be calculated for a particular sector by using the expression

$$r_i = y_i \cdot t - \text{MD}_i \cdot \Delta y c_i \tag{10.8}$$

which gives the return of sector i in terms of its yield, its modified duration, and the elapsed time. Since all these quantities will be known, the change in yield curve can be calculated.

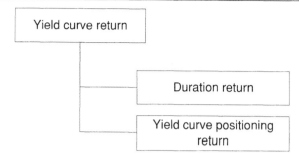

Figure 10.2 Decomposition of yield curve return into duration return and yield curve positioning components

In this case the return that is purely due to duration effects, $r_{duration}$, is given by

$$r_{duration} = \tilde{r}_{yc}^{B} - r_{yc}^{B} \tag{10.9}$$

Other changes in the shape of the yield curve that generate return but that cannot be attributed to duration effects are called yield curve positioning effects. This quantity, $r_{curve\_positioning}$, may be calculated from

$$r_{curve} = r_{yc}^{P} - r_{yc}^{B} - r_{duration} \tag{10.10}$$

Duration attribution can only be calculated at the level at which data is supplied for the benchmark, due to the summation over benchmark sectors in Equation (10.7). This means that, for instance, if benchmark data is only supplied at the sector level, it is not possible to supply portfolio duration attribution returns at the security level.

Duration attribution therefore differs in an important respect from other forms of yield curve attribution, for which a portfolio and a benchmark may have their yield curve-dependent returns decomposed, irrespective of the level at which each has its data supplied; see Figure 10.2.

11

Roll Return

11.1 INTRODUCTION

Consider a case in which yields do not change over time, so that the shape and level of the yield curve remains the same over the holding period. In addition, let's suppose that the curve is normally shaped, with short-term yields lower than long-term yields. This has been the usual state of affairs in western financial markets post-1945.

With these assumptions, the astute investor can use a strategy called *riding the yield curve*. A security is bought with a longer-term maturity. As time passes, the security's maturity falls and its yield decreases due to the shape of the yield curve. Since the yield is falling, its price increases more rapidly than would be the case with a flat yield curve. Eventually, the investor sells the security at a profit.

Opportunities from roll return tend to occur when the yield curve is steeply sloped. Roll return can add a few useful basis points when the markets are quiet. However, if a portfolio is duration-matched against a benchmark that covers all maturities, some short-dated bonds will have to be included, and these may bring down the overall roll return. This is not necessarily the manager's fault.

The manager's decision may be that it is not worth taking a roll bet. If the expected gain is small and the costs, or the risks, of restructuring the portfolio's exposures exceed that expected from a roll position, then roll may be ignored. The investor should not necessarily expect to see outperformance from roll returns; it may simply be too difficult to include a roll position at the same time as other exposures, while meeting overall hedging requirements.

Think of roll return as a useful way to finesse returns when conditions are right. The bulk of returns will probably come from other sources, such as yield curve movements or credit spreads.

11.2 MAXIMIZING ROLL RETURN

Consider the following situation. You have $1MM to invest for 30 days in the money market. Do you

Buy a 30-day bill and hold it to maturity?
Buy a 60-day bill, hold it for 30 days, and sell it as a 30-day bill?
Buy a 90-day bill, hold it for 30 days, and sell it as a 60-day bill?

With the critical assumption that yields will remain constant, the returns from each of these strategies can be calculated by pricing the bill at the appropriate yield. If the manager is confident that the shape of the yield curve will not change, then exposure can be moved to the steepest part of the yield curve in order to maximize returns, since this is the maturity at which yield will show the most expected change.

Unfortunately things are not quite so simple for bonds, or other instruments for which a regular coupon is paid. Consider the yield curve data shown in Table 11.1. A bond is issued

Table 11.1   Sample yield curve

Maturity	Rate (%)
3 months	1.1
2 years	1.7
4 years	2.2
6 years	2.5

with a 6-year maturity. The 6-year rate on the yield curve is 2.5%, so this is the bond's coupon.

After 2 years, the security has become a 4-year bond, while still paying a coupon of 2.5%. However, other new 4-year bonds are paying a coupon of 2.2%, so the bond is worth more since it has a higher return. In principle, one can then sell the instrument at a profit. However, this effect does not last. As the bond approaches maturity its value starts to revert to par. Since the bond has been trading at a premium, its price will decrease until it gets back to par.

There is therefore a turning point in the bond's capital (clean) price at which it stops rising and starts falling. The ideal strategy for a bond investor is to buy before this point and to sell before the bond's value starts to fall. The change of sign will not be seen in the bond's performance, since this includes regular coupon payments; the effect of these is to ensure the bond's performance is always positive, even if it is held over the period in which capital price falls. However, a portfolio's overall performance can be boosted by actively managing securities, and by selling those bonds that are showing lower returns. Calculation of the ideal point at which to sell is complex, but is affected by bond coupon, maturity, yield to maturity, and the expected shape of the yield curve.

11.3   MEASURING ROLL RETURN

How can the effect of roll return be measured? Since negative roll is generated by changes in capital price, the overall (market) return needs to be split into a coupon (accrued interest) component and a capital price component. This can be done quite easily, even in a perturbational context, by setting

$$r_{roll} = \frac{\delta P_{roll}}{P} = \frac{C \delta t}{P} + \frac{(\delta P_{roll} - C \delta t)}{P} \tag{11.1}$$

where

$$\frac{C \delta t}{P} \tag{11.2}$$

is the return due to accrued interest, and

$$\frac{(\delta P_{roll} - C \delta t)}{P} \tag{11.3}$$

is the return due to changes in capital price due to roll return.

The sum of the two returns will always be positive. However, is it as positive as it might be? This second return will show whether the security has been positioned to roll up or roll down the yield curve. If it is negative, then the security has been held beyond the point at which roll return is generating extra income.

11.4   MEASURING THE EFFECT OF ROLL

Yield curves seldom behave in such a convenient manner as described above. For attribution purposes, we need to isolate the returns made by curve roll from other returns made by movements in the curve.

The way to do this is to use the same curve from the beginning of the interval and at the end, and to revalue each security in the portfolio using this curve, taking the change in maturities into account.

Note that the overall roll return will always be positive, because return will be calculated using market prices and including coupons in performance. If a loss arises from adverse yield curve movements, this will show up in the appropriate section. Roll return cannot be attributed to yield or to yield curve movements, and it therefore belongs in a category of its own.

As discussed in previous chapters, it may not be possible to revalue the security from first principles. In this case a better route may be to calculate the change in yield for each security over the calculation interval, and to use a perturbational approach. For a downwards-sloping curve, the change in yield will always be negative, so the effect on performance will be positive. If the curve is inverted, or shows other complex behaviour, then you may see negative roll return.

11.5   SEPARATING ROLL RETURN FROM YIELD CURVE RETURN

In this section we show how to measure the effect of a change in the yield curve on a security's return.

Label the yield curve at time T as Y_T, and the curve at time $T + 1$ as Y_{T+1}. Then the yield of an instrument with maturity M at time T is given by $Y_T(M)$.

To examine the return of an instrument between times T and $T + \delta t$, we will need to calculate the price – and hence the yield – of the instrument at those times. These yields are calculated from the appropriate yield curves, as follows.

Suppose a given security has maturity M years at time T. Then at time $T + \delta t$ the maturity of the instrument will have decreased from M to $M - \delta t$, since we have moved δt years closer to maturity. This means that while the yield of the security at time T is given by $Y_T(M)$, the yield of the same security at time $T + \delta t$ is given by $Y_{T+1}(M - \delta t)$.

This implies that, even if the yield curve is unchanged over the interval $[T, T + \delta t]$, the yield of the security can still change. If the yield curve is positively sloped, the yield of a security with lower maturity will be less than that of a security with higher maturity. In this case the yield of the security will fall and its price will increase. The return due to this price increase is the roll return. For reference, we set

$$\delta y_{\text{roll}} = Y_{T+1}(M - \delta t) - Y_{T+1}(M) \tag{11.4}$$

What if the yield curve does change? In this case, we can measure the effect of the change by holding maturities constant and looking at how the values of Y_T and Y_{T+1} vary over the interval. Yield curve movement is therefore given by

$$\delta y_{\text{curve}} = Y_{T+1}(M) - Y_T(M) \tag{11.5}$$

The total change in yield is therefore given by

$$\delta y = \delta y_{\text{roll}} + \delta y_{\text{curve}} = Y_{T+1}(M - \delta t) - Y_T(M) \tag{11.6}$$

as required.

12

Credit Return

12.1 INTRODUCTION

So far, the discussion of changes in yields has been restricted to the effects of sovereign curves, or those with the very highest credit rating. Such instruments only form a small part of the universe of investment-grade securities. For non-sovereign AAA securities there is another important source of investment return: that of *credit*.

The bulk of investment-grade securities are assigned credit ratings by the major ratings institutions, of which the best known are Moody's, Fitch IBCA and Standard & Poor's (S&P). These ratings lie on a scale between highest credit quality at one end and lowest (default or junk) at the other. The ratings give an indication of the investment risk entailed in holding a particular instrument, and reflect the ability of the security issuer to meet its repayment obligations. Ratings do not indicate a specific probability of default, but defaults on 'AAA' rated US corporate bonds have averaged less than 0.10% per annum, while the equivalent rate for 'BBB' rated bonds was 0.35%, and for 'B' rated bonds 3.0% (Table 12.1).

Securities with lower credit rating will offer a higher yield (or a lower price) to the investor to compensate for the additional risk carried by the security, where the risk includes non-payment of coupons or principal. Despite the additional risk entailed, there are deep, liquid markets in these non-sovereign instruments, and one can construct yield curves for securities with each credit rating. Curves range in risk from AA (just below sovereign grade) to 'unrated' or 'junk', which carry the highest risk and hence trade at a spread of many hundreds of basis points to their duration-matched equivalents on the sovereign curve.

Since credit spreads continually widen or contract according to various economic factors, this is an important additional source of return that can and should be measured when performing attribution analysis on portfolios that contain non-sovereign securities.

12.2 CREDIT SPREAD AND SECURITY-SPECIFIC RETURN

By definition, credit return is always zero for a Treasury instrument. In other words, the yield of a Treasury instrument should always equal its interpolated yield on the corresponding sovereign yield curve.

In fact, most instruments will show a specific spread to their reference yield curve, no matter what their credit rating. This difference is measured by a security-specific (or illiquidity) effect, which is described further in the next chapter. We note here that credit effects are not sufficient to describe all further yield changes of a security.

In addition, we can choose not to run a spread attribution at all. In this case, all yield movements are regarded as caused by a Treasury curve movement, plus a security-specific or liquidity movement. This may be appropriate for a portfolio composed of Treasury-rated securities, but for any portfolio with a proportion of lower-rated instruments it misclassifies an

Table 12.1   Credit rating ranking and correlations

S&P short-term	S&P long-term	Moody's long-term	Moody's short-term
A1+	AAA	Aaa	Prime − 1
A1+	AA+	Aa1	Prime − 1
A1+	AA	Aa2	Prime − 1
A1+	AA−	Aa3	Prime − 1
A1+ or A1	A+	A1	Prime − 1
A1 or A2	A	A2	Prime − 1 or Prime − 2
A1 or A2	A−	A3	Prime − 1 or Prime − 2
A2	BBB+	Baa1	Prime − 2
A2 or A3	BBB	Baa2	Prime − 2 or Prime − 3
A3	BBB−	Baa3	Prime − 2 or Prime − 3
	CCC+	Ba1	Not Prime
	CCC	Ba2	Not Prime
	CCC−	Ba3	Not Prime
		B1	Not Prime
		B2	Not Prime
		B3	Not Prime
		Caa1	Not Prime
		Caa2	Not Prime
		Caa3	Not Prime
		Ca	Not Prime
		C	Not Prime

important source of return, by viewing return made from credit spread effects as made from spread-specific return.

12.3   CURVES AND SECURITIES

It is important to note the dependencies of securities on yield curves. For instance, an AAA-rated bond will be unaffected by changes in the BBB curve. However, a BBB-rated security will be affected by changes in both the AAA curve and the BBB curve to varying degrees. The question of how much movements in the higher-rated curves affect pricing of lower-rated securities is treated in more detail below.

Similarly, changes in the sovereign to healthcare sector curve spreads will not affect the sovereign to transport sector spread, although there may be some correlation due to general economic conditions.

12.4   FINE STRUCTURE CREDIT CURVE MOVEMENT

Just as for sovereign curves, we can fit a model to a credit curve and examine its movements in terms of shift, twist and butterfly motions. If there are several curves driving the performance of the current portfolio, we can fit corresponding models to each, and examine the changes in spread between each in terms of parallel, steepening and curvature movements.

However, this amount of detail may be too much for all but the most dedicated user. Most investors who examine credit return will usually do so with a single figure.

Table 12.2   Returns from a swap curve attribution analysis

Return from a swap curve attribution analysis
Yield return
Treasury curve return
Swap spread return
Liquidity/security-specific return

12.5   DIFFERENT TYPES OF CREDIT ATTRIBUTION

We describe four types of credit attribution:

- credit spread attribution;
- sector curve attribution;
- swap spread attribution;
- country curve attribution.

12.6   SWAP CURVE ATTRIBUTION

Swap curve attribution measures the effect that changes in the spread between a country's Treasury curve and the swap curve have on each security's yield, and hence its return. The user has the choice of using the raw swap curve, or of fitting a model to the curve and thereby being able to examine the effect of shift, twist and curvature movements. In either case the procedure is exactly the same as for the Treasury curve, in that the movement in the swap curve over a given interval generates a change in yield for each security, and this is included in the results of the analysis (see Table 12.2).

12.7   CREDIT CURVE ATTRIBUTION

Credit curve attribution measures the effects on return of yield curves rated below AAA. With careful structuring, it is possible to immunize a portfolio so that it shows almost no returns due to Treasury curve movements, and all its profit from credit shifts. For investors who follow this strategy, detailed credit attribution is of great interest.

Credit curve attribution should be performed as follows.

(1) Select the credit curves to use. While we can, for instance, use a full set of credit curves (Standard & Poor's long-term ratings run AAA, AA+, AA, AA−, A+, A, A−, BBB+, BBB, BBB−, CCC−, CCC, CCC−, Unrated), such a level of detail may be too much for many managers who may prefer to use just AAA, BBB, CCC or even just one curve.

(2) Decide whether to allow higher-rated yield curves to affect lower-rated curves. For instance, there is a strong correlation between movements in the AAA and AA+ curves, and in this case one describes the returns of an AA+-rated security in terms of the contribution made by movements in the AAA curve, and in movements in the AAA–AA+ spread. On the other hand, there may be little or no correlation between movements in the AAA curve and the lowest-rated (junk) instruments, which may trade at a 600 or more basis point spread to Treasuries. In this case it makes little sense to talk about the effect of movements in the Treasury curve on junk bonds, since they behave independently. Such bonds should be treated quite differently

Table 12.3   Sample returns against credit spread categories (i)

Credit rating	BBB-rated bond	Junk bond
AAA shifts	0.5%	0.0%
AAA–BBB spread	0.2%	0.0%
BBB–CCC spread	0.0%	0.0%
UNR shifts	0.0%	1.2%

to other bonds. Their return is governed entirely by movements in the appropriate junk (UNR) curve, not by movements in the Treasury curve or other high-rated curves.

Results for running attribution on such bonds should look as in Table 12.3 (the BBB-rated curve is listed for comparison).

The BBB-rated bond has its return driven by changes in the AAA curve and the AAA–BBB spread. The BBB–CCC spread has no effect, since this applies to instruments with a lower rating. The junk bond has its return affected only by movements in the UNR curve.

The user needs to decide whether each yield curve is affected by movements in higher-rated curves, or whether it moves independently. A more advanced treatment would associate a correlation measure between yield curves, indicating to what degree a curve is affected by other curves with higher credit ratings.

(3) Decide whether to use raw credit curve data, or whether to fit a model curve to each credit curve. In the latter case, the user can measure, for instance, the effects of a steepening in credit shifts.

(4) If the security has a rating corresponding to a credit curve that moves independently of the rest of the market, calculate the change in the security yield by reading off the change in the credit curve at that security's maturity or duration, and *set the Treasury curve return to zero*. Otherwise, start by calculating spread between the first credit curve and the Treasury curve. Then iterate through each credit curve, calculating the effect of the spread between the current curve and the previous one. If raw credit curve data is used, the difference will be a single yield; if a multi-factor model is used, the difference will be a set of shift, twist and curve spreads.

For each credit curve, subtract the net yield change arising from movements in higher-rated curves, thus giving the spread difference instead of the absolute difference. For instance, suppose that at the 5-year maturity point the Treasury curve moved from 5.5% to 6.5%, and the BBB curve moved from 6.2% to 6.7%. A 5-year BBB-rated security's yield will rise by $(6.7\% - 6.2\%) = +0.5\%$. However, the AAA curve has moved by $(6.5\% - 5.5\%) = 1.0\%$, so the BBB spread has actually moved by $(0.5\% - 1.0\%) = -0.5\%$. The overall result (AAA curve movement plus AAA–BBB spread) is the same as the move in the BBB curve, as expected.

A particular problem in running credit attribution is that of mismatches between available credit curves, and the actual ratings of bonds in the managed portfolio. For instance, suppose we have credit curves for AAA, BBB and CCC, but several bonds that are rated BBB– (i.e. one division lower than BBB). How can we perform credit attribution on these bonds without a BBB– curve?

In this case, the procedure should iterate through the available yield curves until it finds the last curve that has a higher credit rating than the current bond. In this case, we will have returns from movements in the AAA curve and from movements in the AAA–BBB spread.

The movement in the BBB–BBB– spread should also contribute some credit return to this bond. However, we do not know how this spread behaves, since we do not have a BBB– curve. We therefore allocate this extra spread return into the bond's liquidity/specific return.

Table 12.4   Sample returns against credit spread categories (ii)

Credit rating	BBB-rated bond	Junk bond	Movements in
AAA shifts	0.5%	0.0%	Curve
AAA–BBB spread	0.2%	0.0%	Spread
BBB–CCC spread	0.0%	0.0%	Spread
UNR shifts	0.0%	0.8%	Curve
Liquidity/security-specific spread shift	0.1%	−0.1%	Spread
TOTAL	0.8%	0.7%	

Table 12.5   Sample returns against credit spread categories, including credit spread decomposition

Credit rating	BBB-rated bond	Junk bond	Movements in
AAA shifts	0.4%	0.0%	Curve
AAA twist	0.1%	0.0%	Curve
AAA curvature	0.0%	0.0%	Curve
AAA–BBB spread shift	0.1%	0.0%	Spread
AAA–BBB spread twist	0.2%	0.0%	Spread
AAA–BBB spread curvature	−0.1%	0.0%	Spread
BBB–CCC spread shift	0.0%	0.0%	Spread
BBB–CCC spread twist	0.0%	0.0%	Spread
BBB–CCC spread curvature	0.0%	0.0%	Spread
UNR shift	0.0%	0.6%	Curve
UNR twist	0.0%	0.1%	Curve
UNR curve	0.0%	0.1%	Curve
Liquidity/security-specific spread shift	0.1%	−0.1%	Spread
TOTAL	0.8%	0.7%	

Table 12.6   Returns from credit curve attribution analysis

Return from a credit curve attribution analysis

Yield return
Treasury curve return
Curve spread return (possibly over several credit ratings)
Liquidity/security-specific return

If credit spread is not decomposed into shift/twist/curvature effects, then the returns for our sample portfolio will appear as in Table 12.4. We have shown a return for liquidity shift, even though this is not part of the credit attribution.

As before, this illustrates the fundamental difference between the way that BBB-rated bonds and junk bonds are treated. The BBB-rated bond's behaviour is determined by movements in the BBB curve and the AAA curve, so return from both sources is shown. However, movements in the Treasury curve do not affect the junk bond's returns. Nor do movements in the BBB curve, or in fact any curve except that for junk securities. This is why the junk bond only shows returns due to movements in the UNR curve.

If the user decides to run a full shift/twist/butterfly attribution, results for the two sample bonds will look as in Table 12.5. The totals by spread category and by totals are the same, but the decomposition gives more detail (see Table 12.6).

Table 12.7   Returns from sector curve attribution analysis

Return from a sector curve attribution analysis
Yield return
Treasury curve return
Sector return
Liquidity/security-specific return

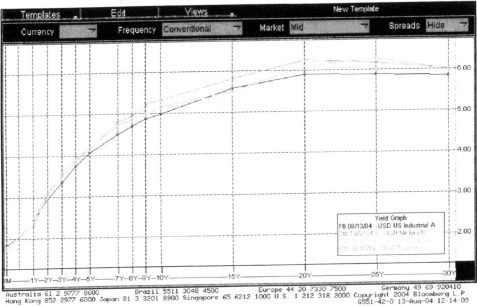

Figure 12.1   A-rated yield curves for USD industrial, media, banking and finance sectors
Used with permission from Bloomberg L.P.

12.8   SECTOR CURVE ATTRIBUTION

Sector curve attribution associates a sector yield curve with each security. Sector yield curves are assigned to market sectors such as healthcare, banks and retail. Only one sector curve can be associated with a given security. Unlike credit curves, sector curves can behave independently and so can cross over and behave in unrelated ways, as in Figure 12.1. If attribution is carried out in this manner, one would show results in terms of broad yield curve movements, then decompose credit spread returns by sector.

Sector curve attribution is performed in exactly the same way as swap or single credit curve attribution. The only difference is that there are multiple sector curves for each country, unlike swap curve attribution, where there is only one swap curve per country (Table 12.7).

12.9 COUNTRY ATTRIBUTION

An important source of return for emerging market bonds is the *country effect*. A USD-denominated bond that is issued by the government of an Asian country into the US domestic market, or the international Eurobond markets, will often trade at a discount to US-issued securities with the same maturity, coupon and credit rating. The higher yield offered by such bonds is informally known as the Yankee premium. Similar terms are used for securities issued in other countries (Samurai bonds are yen-denominated bonds issued in Japan by a non-Japanese borrower, Bulldog bonds are issued in sterling in the UK, Mathilda for Australia, Dragon for a USD-denominated bond issued in Asia, and so on). In general, a Eurobond is a security that is denominated in a currency other than that of the country in which it is issued.

The reason the premium exists is similar to that for the TED spread, defined as the price difference between 3-month futures contracts for US Treasuries and 3-month contracts for Eurodollars having identical expiration months. Although the two contracts are on nominally identical instruments, the market's perception is that the Eurodollar future is intrinsically riskier since it reflects the credit rating of corporate borrowers. The TED spread is therefore a measure of *credit quality*.

For the majority of markets, this country effect is irrelevant since the securities traded will be denominated in the currency of the country of issue. However, there will be some users who have a requirement to measure this country-specific credit spread, particularly those who invest in emerging-country debt.

For instance, consider a BBB-rated Thai Yankee bond that is trading at 100 basis points premium to its USD-issued counterpart, but lies exactly on the Thai USD curve. In this case, the country spread is 100 basis points and the liquidity spread is 0 basis points. Without the ability to measure country effect, the 100 basis points spread will be attributed to liquidity or issuer-specific factors, which may be strictly correct but does not convey any extra information.

The country effect can be included in all standard security-level analyses. When the issuing country's currency is the same as the security currency, the country effect will always be zero. Only for cases where the two differ will the value of the country effect be non-zero. For the Thai example shown above, the security return decomposition will then run as follows:

- yield effect;
- USD Treasury curve movements (shift, twist, butterfly);
- USD credit curve movements (from AAA to BBB);
- country effect (spread from USD BBB to Thai USD curve);
- liquidity or security-specific effect (spread from Thai USD curve to market yield).

This assumes that we have a BBB yield curve for the Thai Eurodollar market. This may not always be the case, since such bonds can form a small proportion of the total number of securities issued. In this case the country effect will be shown as part of the security-specific return (Figure 12.2).

The advantage for the purchaser of such a bond is that exchange rate risk is removed. Against this must be balanced the possibility of higher default risk.

To perform country attribution for such a bond, we require the USD Treasury curves for the country in whose currency the bond is issued, and for the country where the bond was issued.

Table 12.8   Returns from country curve attribution analysis

Return from a country curve attribution analysis
Yield return
Treasury curve return
Country return
Security-specific return

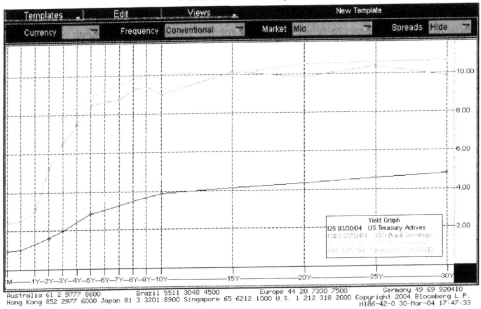

Index **YCRV**

Figure 12.2   Yield curves for US Treasury actives, USD Brazil sovereign, USD Chile sovereign, USD Venezuela government issues. Note the 500 basis point spread between AAA USD bonds issued in the USA and AAA USD bonds issued in Brazil and Venezuela
Used with permission from Bloomberg L.P.

The yield of the instrument due to currency return is then calculated as the difference between the levels of the two yield curves at the appropriate maturity.

Country attribution can be combined with credit curve attribution, sector attribution or swap attribution as in Table 12.8.

13

Optionality Return

Optionality return arises from securities with option-related risk in the current portfolio. Such instruments include:

- naked options;
- options on bonds and futures;
- embedded options in bonds;
- mortgage-backed securities.

For a mortgage-backed security, changes in the option-adjusted spread (OAS) reflect prepayment risk, as distinct from yield curve risk or credit risk. Prepayment risk only applies to mortgage-backed securities (MBS).

The yield of a mortgage-backed security is often given in terms of OAS, such that

$$y = y_T + \text{OAS} \tag{13.1}$$

where y is the yield of the instrument, y_T is the yield of a duration-matched Treasury instrument, and OAS is the option-adjusted spread to the Treasury curve. This spread includes any credit or sector spreads, as well as option-specific spreads. In an attribution framework, it is therefore worth examining how this spread can be decomposed into option-specific and non-option-specific components.

For an MBS, we decompose yield changes into the following components:

$$\delta y = \delta y_T + \delta y_{CR} + \delta y_{OPT} + \delta y_{\text{specific}} \tag{13.2}$$

where δy_T is the change in yield due to Treasury curve movements, δy_{CR} the change in yield due to credit spread shifts, δy_{OPT} the change due to prepayment risk, and $\delta y_{\text{specific}}$ the change in yield due to bond-specific effects.

Combining equations (13.1) and (13.2) gives

$$\delta y - \delta y_T = \delta y_{CR} + \delta y_{OPT} + \delta y_{\text{specific}} = \delta \text{OAS} \tag{13.3}$$

That is, given the change in credit spread and the change in option-adjusted spread, we can isolate the change in yields due to option-specific effects. Note, however, that any bond-specific effects are included in this option-specific yield change.

Other option-related returns can be calculated if we know the changes in other quantities such as volatility. This means that extra terms need to be added into the basic perturbation equation:

$$r = y \cdot \delta t - \text{MD} \cdot \delta y + \tfrac{1}{2} C (\delta y)^2 + \Delta ds + \theta dt + \tfrac{1}{2} (d\gamma)^2 + \xi d\nu \tag{13.4}$$

where:

Δ (delta) is the option's first-order sensitivity to price changes;
γ (gamma) is the option's second-order sensitivity to price changes;

θ (theta) is the option's time-decay sensitivity; and

ζ (vega) is the option's volatility sensitivity.

If one or more of these quantities is not available, the return due to their effect may be set to zero.

A useful worked example for attribution on mortgage-backed securities is given in Hayre (2001, chap. 14).

14

Asset Allocation Return

There are some cases where a bond portfolio's returns should include an asset allocation term, particularly where currency exposures are concerned. This chapter describes the impact of the asset allocation calculation, and what to expect from the results.

There are several practical points to consider in the calculation of asset allocation returns. Firstly, is data supplied at security level or sector level? Whilst we can be confident that portfolio data will have security-level information, this is often not the case for benchmark data. Due to the size of many modern benchmarks, it is simply impractical for many fund managers to record and reprice all the bonds in a benchmark. In this case, benchmark data may be supplied at the country or industry level only (Figure 14.1).

There are three cases to consider.

1. Data is available at security level for both portfolio and benchmark, and the user runs a security-level attribution analysis.
2. Data is available at security level for both portfolio and benchmark, and the user runs a segment-level attribution analysis.
3. Data is available at security level for portfolio and at segment level for benchmark.

In all three cases, it is desirable to show as much data as possible in the final results.

Why do we discriminate between cases 1 and 2? The reason is that, depending on whether we calculate asset allocation return at security or segment level, we can get quite different results. Both are valid, and so it is important to make either type of analysis available.

If asset allocation returns are to be calculated in addition to fixed income attribution effects, the standard equity attribution expression

$$R_{\text{excess}} = \sum_{i \in S} \left(a_i^P - a_i^B \right) r_i^B + \sum_{i \in S} \left(r_i^P - r_i^B \right) a_i^P \tag{14.1}$$

should be used, where the first term measures asset allocation return, the second measures stock selection return, and the summation is over a group of securities or segments.

14.1 CASE 1

Start by calculating the fixed income returns for all securities in the portfolio. Next, calculate security-level asset allocation and selection returns using Equation (14.1). Note that the presence of the a_i^P term in the stock selection expression means that stock selection return is zero for all securities that are in the benchmark but not in the portfolio. For these, the only source of return is asset allocation.

For those securities that have non-zero stock selection return, the stock selection is divided up into the various sources of return from fixed interest effects in a *pro rata* fashion. For instance, if the return of a security was 50% yield return, 25% Treasury curve, 25% credit return, then the stock selection return for this security would be allocated to these sources of

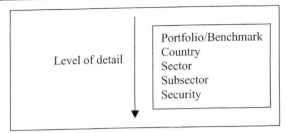

Figure 14.1   Levels of detail in attribution analysis

return in the ratio 50:25:25. Expressed another way, the sum of the fixed interest returns is equal to the stock selection return for securities in the portfolio (note that this ignores trading and price return).

14.2   CASE 2

Again, start by calculating the fixed income returns for all securities in the portfolio and benchmark. Next, calculate segment-level asset allocation returns. This time, we aggregate returns and asset allocations by sector *before* using Equation (14.1). For each segment, we now have an asset allocation return. Lastly, calculate stock selection returns by aggregating each fixed interest return term (such as yield return or Treasury curve return) over the current sector and using these returns to calculate a sector stock selection. For instance, this gives us the yield return for each sector in the portfolio and the benchmark.

In other words, the second term in Equation (14.1) is rewritten

$$R_{SS} = \sum \left(r^P_{yield} - r^B_{yield} \right) \cdot a_P + \sum \left(r^P_{shift} - r^B_{shift} \right) \cdot a_P + \cdots + \sum \left(r^P_{credit} - r^B_{credit} \right) \cdot a_P$$
(14.2)

where the i indices have been omitted for clarity. This gives us all the fixed income returns, summarized by segment. If we want to examine the results at security level, we can display the individual $(r^P_{risk} - r^B_{risk}) \cdot a_P$ terms, and aggregate them by sector.

With this approach we cannot examine asset allocation returns at security level, since they are only available at segment level. This is one of the costs of running a segment-level analysis on security-level data.

14.3   CASE 3

As before, calculate fixed income returns for all securities in the portfolio. In addition, we treat each benchmark segment as a synthetic bond with its own coupon, yield, maturity, modified duration and return. Since this is all the information we need to use the perturbation equation, we can run an attribution analysis on these segments and derive yield, Treasury curve and other returns according to the type of attribution selected.

With these attribution results for the portfolio securities and the benchmark segments, we can follow the approach of case 2. However, since we only have values for r^B_{yield} at the segment level instead of the security level, we cannot show the individual $(r^P_{yield} - r^B_{yield}) \cdot a_P$ terms at the security level. Therefore results can only be displayed as far down as the segment level.

In this case, each benchmark segment is represented as a synthetic instrument, in the same way as a physical instrument. For each segment, the portfolio contains various physical securities, while the benchmark portfolio has exactly one security.

From the argument in case 1, any security that is not represented in the portfolio has a zero stock selection return. At the stock level, this applies to the synthetic instruments in the benchmark, so at the stock level we can only examine fixed income attribution effects on the portfolio instruments. This makes it impossible to compare, say, the relative effect of yield curve shifts on portfolio and benchmark. This is another reason why this analysis only works at the segment level.

15

Other Sources of Return

We have now covered the main sources of return in a fixed income portfolio. This chapter covers a range of remaining effects that were not considered in earlier chapters because they do not fall into any convenient categories.

These remaining sources of return are:

- convexity;
- liquidity;
- trading;
- price;
- residual.

15.1 CONVEXITY RETURN

Convexity return arises from the convexity term in the fundamental perturbation equation:

$$r_{convexity} = \tfrac{1}{2}C(\delta y)^2 \qquad (15.1)$$

Here, δy is the change in market yield of the security over the entire interval. No decomposition of δy into Treasury curve movements or credit spreads is carried out, since convexity return is typically small.

15.2 LIQUIDITY (SECURITY-SPECIFIC) RETURN

Liquidity return is the remaining change in a security's yield when all other sources of change, including Treasury curve shifts, credit shifts and optionality, have been taken into account. Particularly when credit curves are fitted to smoothing functions, the actual market yield of the instrument is unlikely to lie exactly on the curve, and this difference is one source of liquidity returns.

Other causes are:

- securities being bid or offered in the repo market;
- securities being bid for coupon-related tax reasons;
- genuine market illiquidity, for which the market will demand a higher yield;
- inadequate modelling of the causes of a security yield change;
- market noise.

To give an example of the sorts of liquidity effects that may be seen in the Australian market, consider the case of a DSL 6.25% 15/11/06 bond. This is similar in all respects to a Commonwealth government 15/11/2006 bond: they have the same maturity and credit rating, and so we would expect them to trade at roughly the same yield. Yet on 20th June 2003 the closing yield for this bond was 4.655%, against a closing yield of 4.255% for its government-backed counterpart – a spread of 40 basis points.

The reason the spread exists is that the market perceives the DSL bond as being an inherently riskier investment than its Treasury counterpart because of liquidity issues. The issue size for the DSL bond was $500MM AUD, while the issue size of the CGL bond was $6102MM AUD – more than 10 times higher. Although the default risk is assessed as being the same in both cases, the market demands a higher return from the corporate bond because its lower issue volume in the marketplace implies that it will be harder to enter into, or exit from a position in the bond; dealing spreads are therefore wider. We refer to this extra premium as *liquidity spread*.

In addition, liquidity return is a catch-all term for the other sources of return listed, which are very difficult to separate. These remaining effects are expected to be small.

15.3   TRADING AND PRICE RETURN

Trading return is the extra value added or subtracted by dealing at prices that are different to end-of-day revaluation rates. If no trades are performed during a given interval, then the trading return will be zero over that interval. However, if a trader has the skill to choose advantageous levels at which to buy and sell securities, then this will add extra returns to the portfolio.

Price return allows us to measure the effect of using different prices to revalue identical securities held in the portfolio and the benchmark. Typically, this occurs when the benchmark vendor uses one set of prices to revalue the benchmark, but the manager uses a different set of prices from a different source. Price return can be an important source of return in equity portfolios.

Trading and price return are closely related and we treat them together. In this section, r refers to the return of security or sector i at time t.

Denote:

r_{Dietz} as the local return, including trading effects. This return should always be available for securities in the portfolio, since it may be calculated directly using end-of-day rates;

r_{P} as the return of the security, calculated using portfolio prices – this may not be available; $\mathbf{r_B}$ as the return of the security, calculated using benchmark prices – if this is available, it will be supplied by the benchmark data vendor.

We do not assume that r_{P} or r_{B} are available. If not, then trading and price return may not be available.

Define price return, r_{price}, as

$$r_{\text{price}} = r_{\text{p}} - r_{\text{B}} \tag{15.2}$$

for securities that exist in both the portfolio and benchmark (r_{price} is zero by definition for securities that do not exist in either the portfolio or benchmark). Price return measures return generated by mispricing of the same security in portfolio and benchmark. If data for either or both r_{P} and r_{B} is unavailable, then price return is always zero.

Next, denote trading return, r_{trading}, as

$$r_{\text{trading}} = r_{\text{Dietz}} - r_{\text{P}} \tag{15.3}$$

If r_{P} is unavailable, use r_{B} instead. If r_{B} is unavailable, then trading return is zero since it cannot be calculated. Trading return measures the extra return over and above a reference return that is generated by cash flows in and out of the portfolio. The two terms r_{price} and r_{trading} may be calculated independently.

Even if benchmark data is only supplied at sector level, we can still calculate a sector-level trading return. To do this, we compare the sector-level Dietz return for the portfolio against the sector-level return for the benchmark. The difference is the trading return for the sector. In such a situation, price return cannot be calculated so it should always be set to zero.

15.4   RESIDUAL RETURN

Residual return is the difference between a security's price change due to yield changes, and its price change in the market. For any given security, residual return is given by

$$r_{residual} = r_{Dietz} - r_{price} - r_{trading} - r_{yield} - r_{spread} - r_{specific} \qquad (15.4)$$

In effect, residual return is the difference between the actual return of the security and the return calculated by adding up all known effects. Residual return should be small or zero in all cases.

16

Worked Examples

Consider a US Treasury bond with maturity date 30th September 2007, coupon 7.5%. On date 30th September 2002 this bond has a yield of 5.8% and a market price of $107.287816 per $100 FV. At date 31st October 2002 the bond has a yield of 5.7% and a market price of $108.256068 per $100 FV. The modified duration and convexity at 30th September are 4.1695 and 21.1033, respectively.

16.1 EXAMPLE 1: YIELD RETURN AND TERM STRUCTURE RETURN

Let's first decompose this bond's return in terms of yield return and term structure return. Over the 31 days between 30-Sep and 31-Oct, the return of the bond due to yield is

$$r_{yield} = \frac{31}{365} \times 5.8\% = 0.4926\% \tag{16.1}$$

This is the return we would expect the bond to have if yields had not changed over the interval. In fact, the yield has fallen slightly, so the yield return will be very slightly less than this amount.

Next, let's calculate the return of the bond due to yield curve changes. The yield of this bond has fallen by 0.1%. We use the standard perturbation equation

$$\delta P = \left[-MD \cdot \delta y + \frac{C(\delta y)^2}{2} \right] P \tag{16.2}$$

to calculate how the price of a security changes when yields vary by an amount δy, where P is the market price, δP is the change in market price, MD is the modified duration and C the convexity of the security. Since

$$r_{price} = \frac{\delta P}{P} \tag{16.3}$$

this equation also gives us the return due to term structure changes.

In this case

$$r_{price} = (-4.1695 \times -0.1\%) + (21.1033 \times -0.1\% \times -0.1\% \div 2) \tag{16.4}$$

giving

$$r_{price} = 0.4180\% \tag{16.5}$$

The overall return of this bond is therefore

$$r_{total} = 0.4926\% + 0.4180\% = 0.9106\% \tag{16.6}$$

This is close (within 0.008%) to the true value of 0.9025%. In fact, if we had used the yield at the end of the interval rather than the beginning, the overall return would become 0.9021%, which is even closer. The difference arises because of variations in yield and compounding rates across the 31-day interval over which the bond's performance is being calculated.

16.1.1   Decomposing returns

In any performance measurement and system, it is vitally important that existing returns figures are not distorted by an attribution analysis. For instance, if the return of the bond in Example 1 is calculated as 0.9025% by the back office, then the sum of attribution effects for this bond must add up to precisely this figure. However, because of residual and other approximation effects, we will seldom see an exact match.

A straightforward solution is to adjust each return figure so that this condition is fulfilled. For example, we set

$$r_{\text{yield}} = \frac{0.9025\%}{0.9106\%} \times 0.4926\% = 0.4882\% \tag{16.7}$$

$$r_{\text{price}} = \frac{0.9025\%}{0.9106\%} \times 0.4180\% = 0.4143\% \tag{16.8}$$

In this way the relative contributions of each risk component are maintained, and overall returns remain correct.

16.2   EXAMPLE 2: YIELD RETURN AND DETAILED TERM STRUCTURE RETURN

In this second example, we decompose the yield change in more detail. More detailed attribution analysis requires that we take a closer look at the sources of the yield change in Equation (16.2). In this second example, we decompose yield movements into changes in the Treasury curve and credit spread movements.

The Nelson–Siegel coefficients for the Treasury yield curve on 30-Sep-2002 are (6.0424504, -1.236457, -1.168738); on 31-Oct-2002 they are (6.2801126, -1.531751, -1.669198). These numbers are calculated by plotting the Treasury par yield curve against bond maturities, and performing a least-squares fit of the equation

$$R(m) = \beta_0 + (\beta_1 + \beta_2)\frac{[1 - \exp(-m)]}{m} - \beta_2 \exp(-m) \tag{16.9}$$

at both dates.

On 30-Sep-2002 the maturity of the bond is 5.0027 years, and on 31-Oct-2002 it is 4.9178 years.

The zero-order, or parallel shift, component of the bond's yield shift can now be calculated by evaluating Equation (16.9) with β_1 and β_2 terms set to zero at both dates, maturities as in the previous paragraph, and calculating the difference between the terms. This reduces to

$$\delta y_{\text{shift}} = \beta_0^{t=1} - \beta_0^{t=0} = 0.2377\% \tag{16.10}$$

In other words, the Treasury curve has moved upwards across all maturities by about 24 basis points.

The first-order, or twist, component of this bond's shift also follows from Equation (16.9). This time we set the β_2 term to zero, and calculate how the yield curve has shifted when shift and twist components are included. Substituting the numbers into Equation (16.9) again gives

$$\delta y_{\text{shift+twist}} = 5.9709\% - 5.7970\% = 0.1739\% \tag{16.11}$$

Subtracting the portion of this change due to shift movements gives

$$\delta y_{\text{shift}} = -0.0638\% \tag{16.12}$$

so the Treasury curve has flattened by about six basis points at the point corresponding to this bond's maturity.

The second-order, or butterfly, component follows in a similar manner. Using all β components in Equation (16.9) gives

$$\delta y_{\text{shift+twist+butterfly}} = 5.6462\% - 5.5728\% = 0.0734\% \tag{16.13}$$

Subtracting the portion of this change due to shift and twist movements gives

$$\delta y_{\text{butterfly}} = -0.1006\% \tag{16.14}$$

These three changes account for $+7$ basis points of the bond's yield change over the interval. However, the yield of the bond actually fell by 10 basis points. This means that credit spreads tightened substantially (by -0.1734%) over the interval.

Check: total yield movement is 0.2377% -0.0638% -0.1006% $-0.1734\% = -0.1001\%$

Now that the yield movement has been broken down into its various components, we can again use Equation (16.2) to calculate their effects on the bond's performance.

The yield return remains as calculated in Example 1, at 0.4926%. Other returns are given by

$$r_{\text{shift}} = (-4.1695 \times 0.2377\%) = -0.9911\%$$
$$r_{\text{twist}} = (-4.1695 \times -0.0638\%) = 0.2660\%$$
$$r_{\text{butterfly}} = (-4.1695 \times -0.1006\%) = 0.4195\%$$
$$r_{\text{credit}} = (-4.1695 \times -0.1734\%) = 0.7230\%$$
$$r_{\text{convexity}} = 21.1034 \times -0.1\% \times -0.1\% \times -0.1\% \div 2 = 0.00105\%$$

giving a total yield curve return of 0.4180%, as in Example 1.

In this case we have moved returns due to the convexity term in (16.2) into a separate, convexity return. The reason for separating out the convexity terms is that:

(i) they are always small, and it is more straightforward to group them all in a single convexity contribution term;
(ii) if they are included in the return calculation for each source of risk, the non-linear δy^2 term means that we get slightly different results, according to the level of yield decomposition (by isolating the convexity return, we always get exactly the same overall return, irrespective of the level of attribution).

Part III

Fixed Income Attribution in Practice

17
Implementing an Attribution System

17.1 BUILD OR BUY?

The track record of banking institutions on building attribution systems is not good. Before you think of writing such a system in-house, give some careful thought to the implications and risks of the buy/build decision.

This chapter is a checklist of factors to consider when deciding whether to build or buy an attribution system. Every case is different and I won't give a hard and fast set of recommendations. We do, however, recommend you give some consideration to the points raised here; they are all based on hard-won experience.

17.2 MATCH TO EXISTING INVESTMENT PROCESS

Does the proposed software match your existing process? For instance, are you trying to use an equity-style attribution system to assess the results of fixed income investment decisions? More broadly, is the proposed system capable of giving your traders the information they need and expect?

17.3 CAN THE ATTRIBUTION APPROACH BE EXTENDED?

If your investment strategy is likely to make heavy use of (for instance) credit derivatives, can the proposed software solution give you the appropriate feedback on the sorts of decision made? Can the approach handle new types of instrument with new risk dependencies?

17.4 PERFORMANCE CALCULATION ENGINE

Accurate attribution relies on an accurate performance calculation. As mentioned previously, I suggest using performance data from an existing back-office application; this will be definitive and you will not need to run reconciliation checks. Try to get as much detail as possible, over time and over security; remember that you cannot repartition data if you do not have it available at the security level.

What if you really want to write a calculation engine in-house, and you are prepared for the data maintenance and reconciliation issues? By the time you have acquired the expertise to put an attribution system together, you will almost certainly have the ability to write a performance engine in a third-generation language such as C or C++. If you are sure that your local experts will remain in-house, you may wish to follow this route; or performance engines can be outsourced. Don't forget to handle work-flow issues involving backdating of trades.

17.5   INTEGRATION WITH OTHER SYSTEMS

Elsewhere in this book we have written of the need to integrate attribution analysis with risk control and analysis. This requires close integration of the two functions, which at least until recently may have been regarded as separate. In particular, risk is seen as a front- and middle-office function, with performance and attribution belonging in the back office. Is it possible to provide integration of these functions within your existing environment?

Does the system store the information you require for attribution (for instance, yield curve data, links from securities to yield curves)? If not, you will need to maintain this data elsewhere, and update it when necessary (such as when a new security is bought in). This means that two sets of data need to be maintained; one in the existing performance system, and one in the attribution system. It is vital to ensure data consistency.

17.6   BENCHMARK AND DATA ISSUES

Data acquisition is by far the most time-consuming and frustrating issue involved in attribution. You may find a software vendor who makes benchmarks available; this is a plus. The questions to ask when looking for sources of pricing and benchmark data are the following.

- Are benchmarks well defined and documented? Can the constituent stocks and prices (including capital price and accrued interest) be downloaded?
- Can the data vendor recreate index returns from the raw data – including stock splits, stock code changes, estimated versus actual dividends, and coupons?
- Are historical rates available in case your download procedure misses a day?
- Can you check the calculated day's returns for each sector against the published returns – every day? This is both labour-intensive and data-intensive, but critical until validated data sets become available.

If the answer to any of these questions is 'no', then be careful. Nothing devours time and resources as much as replication benchmark returns; and even if the results are 99.9% correct, they remain 100% wrong.

17.7   REPORTING

To get the maximum leverage from attribution analysis requires extensive display and interpretation capabilities for multi-dimensional data. Dimensions include:

- time (day, week, month, quarter, year);
- risk (asset allocation, stock selection, trading skill, yield curve decisions, FX changes);
- sector (market, sub-sector, sector, portfolio).

Typically the user will have to wade through numerous paper reports to interpret what's going on.

Even if you are buying a third-party solution, consider developing an OLAP (On-Line Analytical Processing) interface that allows the user to interact with data, slice and dice, drill down, and so on. Your users will love you for it.

17.8   IT REQUIREMENTS

Our advice is: don't use a spreadsheet for anything but the most ad hoc, one-off attribution analysis. David Spaulding labours this point at length in his book, and he is wholly correct to do so (Spaulding, 2003b).

If you start writing attribution tools in desktop databases such as Access, there will inevitably come a point at which the application will need to migrate to an industrial-strength database such as Oracle or SQL Server. Save yourself time, cost and effort, and do it right the first time. There is no way around the IT requirements for performance and attribution calculation: every attribution system requires a professional, industrial-strength database.

If you are maintaining a proper set of indices and benchmarks, even for front-office use, there will be a substantial amount of data requiring a client–server database such as Oracle or SQL Server. This means hiring a database administrator, or having someone around who can fill this role.

17.9   COST

This includes staff costs, data costs, IT costs, licensing costs. Remember the old adage, 'You can have it good, cheap or quick – any two'.

17.10   TIME

Some of the major vendors of performance and attribution systems quote a standard 6-month deployment period for an 'off-the-shelf' international equity attribution system. This translates to extra costs.

17.11   MANAGEMENT SUPPORT

In our experience, any successful attribution system needs a senior individual in the hosting organization who is both convinced of the necessity for attribution and has the influence to push through the costs. Attribution systems are not suitable for skunk-work type projects; they are simply too visible and too resource-hungry.

17.12   INTELLECTUAL CAPITAL

Do you have the staff resources to build such a system? Attribution is a complex business. Building an attribution system requires the following (Figure 17.1).

- *Mathematical knowledge*: Specifically, the mathematics of performance calculation, attribution, the approximations inherent in performance measurement, the role of residuals, instrument pricing, yield curve calculation.
- *Computing knowledge*: The ability to translate mathematical papers and concepts into working, reliable systems; expert knowledge of client–server databases; expert knowledge of a 3GL such as C++; ability to optimize systems and decide, for instance, which portions of a system should run as SQL queries and which should run on the client machine.

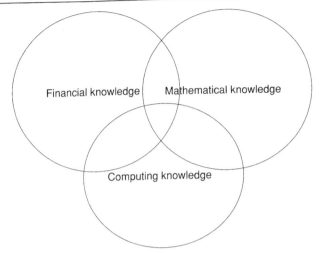

Figure 17.1   Overlapping skills required to build an attribution system.

- *Finance*: An understanding of a fund manager's requirements and industry standards, where relevant; knowledge of industry benchmarks and standards; ability to liaise with all levels of a fund manager's organization; the specifics of each type of market traded, such as stock splits, dividend payments, security name changes for equities; the role of CPI-related pricing inputs for indexed bonds and annuities; and so on.

We need hardly point out that this is not a common mixture of skills, particularly in a single individual. Unless you are extremely fortunate, don't expect your summer intern to knock up an industrial-strength attribution system – and if you do, make sure you can get him back later.

17.13   INTERFACE TO LEGACY SYSTEMS

Most institutions will need to keep running their legacy performance measurement systems in tandem with the new attribution systems. This is not necessarily a problem – as long as proper procedures can be put in place and adequately staffed.

How easy is it to extract data from the legacy system? Does it record benchmark data at the required level of detail (or at all)? If not, you may need to integrate data from the legacy application and at least one source of external data.

17.14   USER EXPECTATIONS

Don't raise the expectations of your users too much. Under-promise and over-deliver.

17.15   IN GENERAL...

As with most projects the smart approach is to leave as much of the work as possible to someone else. The rest of the decision has to be based on the skills and resources available within your organization. In spite of all the warnings in this chapter, don't write off in-house development if you feel you have assessed the up-front and hidden costs.

18

_____ Fixed Income Benchmarks _____

18.1 INTRODUCTION

Benchmarks merit a chapter to themselves, as they can take up a substantial proportion of an attribution analyst's time.

A benchmark is a reference portfolio of instruments, that has its holdings adjusted typically once a month, with a composition governed by a set of pre-defined rules. Despite this transparent-sounding description, in practice benchmarks are one of the most time-consuming requirements for fixed income attribution.

There are several reasons for this.

1. Benchmarks can be very large.
2. Benchmark security definition data is often difficult to find.
3. Pricing assumptions for benchmark securities are often unclear.

In addition, consider the types of behaviour that one must model in order to reproduce a benchmark.

- As bonds mature, they drop out of the index.
- As new bonds are issued, they must be assessed to decide whether they fit the inclusion criteria to be included in the benchmark.
- At pre-defined intervals, the composition of benchmarks changes to reflect changes in the market weights on issue of each security. This interval is usually monthly, but can be weekly for bill indices.
- Benchmarks show intra-month cash flows arising from coupon payments and security maturities.
- There are complex rules that govern how cash arising from coupon payments and maturities should be reinvested in the index.
- Bonds also enter or leave the benchmark depending on the benchmark's definition; for instance, over a given month a 3–5-year index may well have bonds entering (as their maturity drops below 5 years during the month) or leaving (as their maturity drops below 3 years).

Benchmarks can range in size from just a few bonds to many thousands. As well as vanilla bonds, there exist benchmarks for virtually every fixed income asset class.

Fund managers often carve out parts of benchmarks, and mix and match benchmarks to match their stated requirements. For instance, a mandate might require that a fund is managed with respect to a synthetic benchmark composed of 50% the UBSW Bank Bill index and 50% the 1+ years UBSW Government index. The 1+ years index is simply composed of those bonds that have greater than 1 year to run to maturity. Bonds with less than this time to run to maturity are removed from the index at the appropriate date.

Table 18.1   Sample benchmark performance data

Index name	1-Month performance (%)	3-Month performance (%)	12-Month performance (%)
Megabank Corporate Bond Index 0+	5	7	9
Megabank Corporate Bond Index 0–3 years	1	2	3
Megabank Corporate Bond Index 3–5 years	1	2	4
Megabank Corporate Bond Index 5–10 years	2	2	0
Megabank Corporate Bond Index 15+ years	1	1	2

So why are benchmarks important in attribution? A fund manager's benchmark requirements for performance measurement are relatively straightforward. Benchmark index values allow the performance of a benchmark to be calculated over any given interval, and this information is widely available for the majority of benchmarks. Availability of raw performance data seldom causes difficulties. Benchmark requirements for fixed income attribution, however, are quite a different problem! Benchmark returns are affected by all the effects that govern performance of a managed portfolio, with the exception of trading return and price return. In order to run attribution correctly, one needs as much detail as possible about the current benchmark in order to calculate the effects of yield curve changes. While the performance analyst only needs a single time series for benchmark performance, the attribution analyst needs daily stock-level performance, risk and return figures. *Data requirements for attribution are therefore orders of magnitude larger.*

18.2   BENCHMARK REPLICATION

Selection of bonds to be included in a benchmark is a skilled task. Bonds should be liquid, actively traded, redeemable for cash, and they must not appeal to domestic investors for local tax or regulatory reasons. It should be possible to replicate the index in practice, using a subset of the bonds from the benchmark. However, benchmarks are usually provided by banks, so why should they cause any difficulties?

The reason is that very often one has to work with incomplete information about benchmarks. One of the main reasons is that, at least until recently, the only requirement for a benchmark was knowledge of its overall returns, its risks and (perhaps) its sector returns.

Unfortunately, benchmark data is often restricted to an accumulation index for an overall index, without any market capitalization data. The sort of data that is typically available is as given in Table 18.1. This data is insufficient for attribution analysis, even if all we want to do is partition the benchmark by maturity buckets. The reason is that the market capitalization – and hence the relative weights of the sectors – are not given.

However, the main problem with security-level benchmark data supplied by most vendors is that rates of return are not available. To calculate the returns of individual securities, one needs to know their prices and cash flows. This in turn requires knowledge of the pricing formula used, the ex-coupon conventions, any non-standard features such as non-uniform first coupon payments, and so on. Unfortunately, this information is not always made available.

Hopefully this situation will change in future, and benchmark vendors will start to supply their data in machine-readable, attribution-friendly, validated format. With the growth in attribution requirements, vendors who take a lead in this area will probably see their benchmark usage rise due to the lower costs of using such benchmarks.

18.3   AVAILABILITY OF DATA

At the time of writing, there are peculiar contradictions in the way that the fund management industry handles benchmarks.

Firstly, benchmark data is a considerable source of business risk. For instance, suppose we have a portfolio indexed to its benchmark. The benchmark is realigned so that its modified duration shortens by 0.2 of a year, but the portfolio is not. If the yield curve moves by 50 basis points, the performance difference is $-0.2 \times 0.005 = 10$ basis points – a considerable (and embarrassing) difference to explain away for an indexed fund. If the benchmark is not updated in time for the discrepancy to be noted and the portfolio readjusted, considerable sums of money can be lost.

Accurate, timely data – not just at the summary level, but at the segment and preferably the security level – is therefore critically important to fund managers. Recently, most have seemed to get by with summarized and (sometimes) bucket-by-bucket matching, but under the harsh light that attribution analysis will throw on their returns, this will not be enough. For proper, detailed analysis, benchmarks must be replicated at the security level on a daily basis.

Secondly, benchmark data is hard to obtain. So why is this not achieved in practice? The reason is that benchmarks do not arise out of thin air; they are constructed and maintained by major banks, who use them as marketing tools. Instead of the information being freely disseminated, it is restricted to selected customers of these banks.

This is quite understandable, since these banks go to considerable time and expense in maintaining databases of benchmark prices and yields. These databases are then treated as sources of revenue.

However, this secrecy leads to some difficult situations. For instance, it is often problematic to reproduce benchmark returns from first principles. I have worked on at least one equity benchmark database where it proved impossible to reproduce the overall (published) accumulation returns due to internal inconsistencies in the (published) price returns, cash flows and weights of the constituent securities. Transparency is most important, not just for price data but also for the aggregation algorithms.

One needs an existing relationship with a benchmark publisher to have timely access to changes in the make-up of their benchmarks. Even then, benchmark data is not always provided in computer-friendly form, and several days of effort each month can be required to update even a small institution's benchmarks.

The benchmark publisher frequently does not make end-of-day prices or yields available, so the portfolio manager has to use their own source of data. This leads to the appearance of price return: a spurious return term caused by using different end-of-day prices between portfolio and benchmark.

The contradiction then is that fund managers need more and more detailed benchmark information, but that the providers of this information are not always providing it. We therefore have the odd situation that many fund managers spend a large amount of effort duplicating index calculations that have already been performed inside the benchmark supplier's computer.

Are there solutions to this situation? We believe so, but they may take time to achieve. Firstly, market forces may encourage fund managers to move to benchmarks for which full information is readily accessible. If the effort required in maintaining a set of benchmarks requires several full-time expert staff, but a rival benchmark makes this information fully available, validated and ready to import directly into the attribution system, there will be an inevitable pressure to move to the second benchmark.

Secondly, we may see a change in the format of published benchmark data. For instance, it would be of enormous benefit for this information to be made available in a common machine-readable format, providing returns and asset weights at the security and sector levels, with a validated set of procedures allowing one to reproduce published sector and benchmark returns from security-level data. The data provider would be fully entitled to charge for the effort required in preparing this data, in the knowledge that it would lead to lower business risk and total cost of ownership for purchasers. A smaller fund manager might not require full security-level data; in this case, they might instead decide to purchase sector-level data only, at a commensurate cost.

Thirdly, instead of supplying security prices (which are of limited use for attribution), banks might instead choose to supply security returns. If one wanted the actual prices, they could be made available under a separate agreement.

In the meantime, there are plenty of employment opportunities for persons with experience in setting up benchmarks.

18.4   REPLICATING BENCHMARK RETURNS FROM DATA

Suppose that we have access to benchmark data at the security level. Benchmark vendors tend to provide benchmark data in the form of daily holdings files at the security level, containing security identifiers (such as ISIN codes), security names, prices, face values and market values, and often other data, such as modified duration and spreads to a local reference curve (Table 18.2). Perhaps surprisingly, the main problem in replication of fixed income benchmark returns

Table 18.2   Sample benchmark data for a single bond

Code	Sample
Date	4-June-04
ISIN	XX0123456789
Description	Megabank 5.5% 1-Sep-2004
Currency	EUR
Issue	1-Sep-97
Maturity	1-Sep-04
Redemption price	100
Coupon type	2
Frequency	2
First coupon	
Date	1-Jun-98
Start date	1-Mar-04
Coupon	2.75
Daycount convention	ACT/ACT
Spread (CCT)	0.15
Market price	101.052
Accrued	0.725
Capital price	100.777
YTM	2.6135
Duration	0.22591
Convexity	0.2727
Amount (millions)	5605
Weight	0.85598

lies in the calculation of coupon timing and amounts. The timing of coupons depends on the bond issuer, the ex-period convention used and the frequency of coupons. In addition, the amount of coupon paid can depend on whether the bond has a non-standard first coupon period, in which case the first coupon may be more or less than the standard payment. The same considerations may apply to the final coupon payment.

In principle, these coupons may be recalculated from first principles if we know the inception date, first and last coupon dates, maturity date, annual coupon payment and coupon frequency, and ex-day convention for each bond. In practice, this imposes a substantial burden on the index calculator, who has to obtain and verify large amounts of bond data. In addition, the ex-day conventions for many bonds are obscure. While most of these problems can be corrected by manual inspection, this approach is impractical for indices containing very large numbers of bonds. There is no easy answer to these problems, and the reader is advised to consult an expert in this field for more information and assistance. Of course, if benchmark providers published their daily security-level rates of return, these problems would disappear.

18.5   TREATMENT OF CASH

Another complication in benchmark replication is the treatment of cash. When a benchmark coupon is paid or a security matures, the benchmark vendor may either decide to place the resulting cash into a holding account (which will decrease the benchmark's modified duration) or to reinvest it in the benchmark's other securities.

Unfortunately, the exact treatment of such cash flows is often obscure. The author has found that in practice such cash adjustments can usually be ignored, as their impact on the portfolio's calculated return is negligible compared to its published return.

19

Presenting Attribution Results

19.1 INTRODUCTION

One of the major difficulties in displaying attribution data is that a large amount of inter-related data must be made available to the user at the same time. As the previous chapters have shown, attribution data can only be interpreted as an interaction between term structure movements, other sources of risk and the active risk structure of the portfolio, and to make sense of these results requires that this data be presented in a form that allows rapid interpretation of the causes and effects within the portfolio and benchmark.

One major problem is that the dimensionality of the results means that, frequently, trying to decompose returns into single sets of numbers can lead to gross oversimplification. Better insight can often be gained by comparing risks and rewards in graphical format. Presenting attribution results therefore becomes a problem in graphical design and ergonomics.

In this chapter we examine conventional and innovative ways of presenting attribution data in both numerical and graphical formats.

19.2 REPORTING FORMATS

Attribution results need to be shown in different formats, depending on who uses them. For presentation of investment results to asset managers and external investors, a summary showing results is probably appropriate, on suitably glossy brochures, and at fairly long intervals. For the fund manager, a very different approach is needed to show the same results. This individual is using attribution reports as a means to provide frequent feedback on the success of investment decisions and the risk-hedging built into his portfolios. In other words, he wants to ensure that (i) the active risks taken are in fact generating return and (ii) other sources of risk are not generating any return, either positive or negative. This requires much more comprehensive reporting tools.

In general, there are several requirements for such a reporting system. Firstly, it must be *easy to use*, so that the causes of any underperformance can be rapidly isolated. The best attribution system in the world is no good if it simply provides a series of security-level attribution returns, without the ability to combine these in a sensible way. Secondly, it must be *interactive*. For a portfolio with potentially hundreds of bonds, it is counterproductive to produce security-level attribution returns at the outset. A much better approach is to allow the user to take a top-down view of the data, and to drill down through various levels of hierarchical risk and sector returns on attribution results. This allows underperforming curve movements, sector exposure or security underperformance to be isolated in a natural and rapid way. Thirdly, it must be *flexible*. The sources of risk in any fixed income portfolio are many, and the reporting system should be configurable enough to reflect this. A reporting system that has been hard-coded to display shift, twist and butterfly returns may not do nearly so well on credit shifts unless allowed by the system.

This chapter shows several ways in which to achieve these aims.

19.3   PRESENTING NUMERICAL DATA

19.3.1   Paper reports

Traditionally, reports have been delivered on paper. The traditional approach of delivering a performance report is sufficient, but attribution requires so much more information that this is not an optimal approach. A set of reports that covers every situation likely to be met is going to require a large amount of paper – and much of it will be wasted. After all, why bother looking at a security-level curve report, if the sector results are running as expected?

This suggests some form of interactive reporting, which in turn may need new investment in interactive reporting tools.

19.3.2   On-line reporting

With the advent of corporate intranets, on-demand web-based reporting is now an option for many institutions. This meets many of the above requirements. Due to the specialized nature of much attribution information, it may make more sense to buy a pre-developed set of reports from a vendor than to develop them in-house. However, close familiarity with the report suite will still be a necessity to get the best out of the system. If the user needs credit returns broken down by credit sector and maturity bucket, he will have to know where to look.

19.3.3   OLAP technology

A third option – and one the author believes will grow in importance for attribution reporting over the next few years – is the use of OLAP interfaces.

As a case study, Figures 19.1 to 19.5 show the interface for Sienna, an early fixed income attribution system written by the author. The program made extensive use of a third-party OLAP control. OLAP stands for 'On-Line Analytical Processing' and is largely concerned with summarization of data in databases so that it can be shown in many different ways. You won't go very far in a study of OLAP without hearing the terms *slice and dice* and *drilldown*, and these are illustrated in what follows.

Initially, the display shows summarized performance figures for a selected portfolio against its benchmark between two selected dates (Figure 19.1). Double-clicking on the display shows the active return for the portfolio.

The user can drill down into the display by clicking on various points on the screen. By clicking on the Date box, the returns are shown on a daily basis, instead of being aggregated over time (Figure 19.2).

By clicking on the Maturity box, the returns are decomposed by maturity bucket. In this example the program shows performance contributions, rather than absolute performance of each bucket. This was felt to be preferable as it conveyed more information about the sources of return in the portfolio (Figure 19.3).

From this point the user can expand the holdings of each maturity box to drill down to the return contributions of individual securities. Returns can be decomposed in numerous different ways, by modified duration buckets, country, credit rating and instrument type. Further, decompositions can be nested, so that returns can be decomposed by country and then by credit rating, or vice versa.

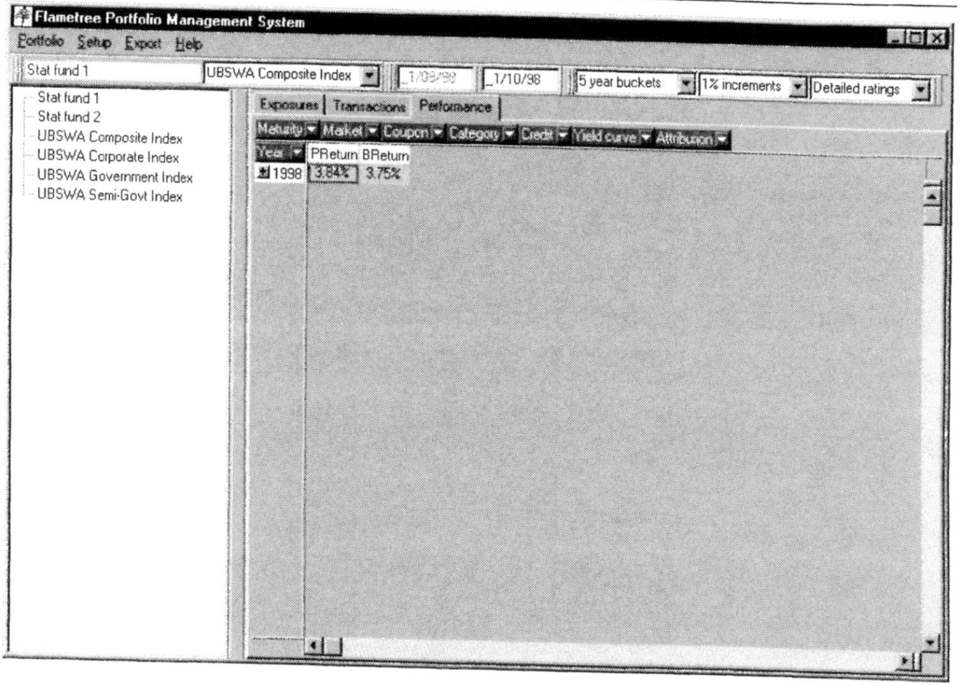

Figure 19.1   Sample OLAP display: summarized performance for portfolio and benchmark

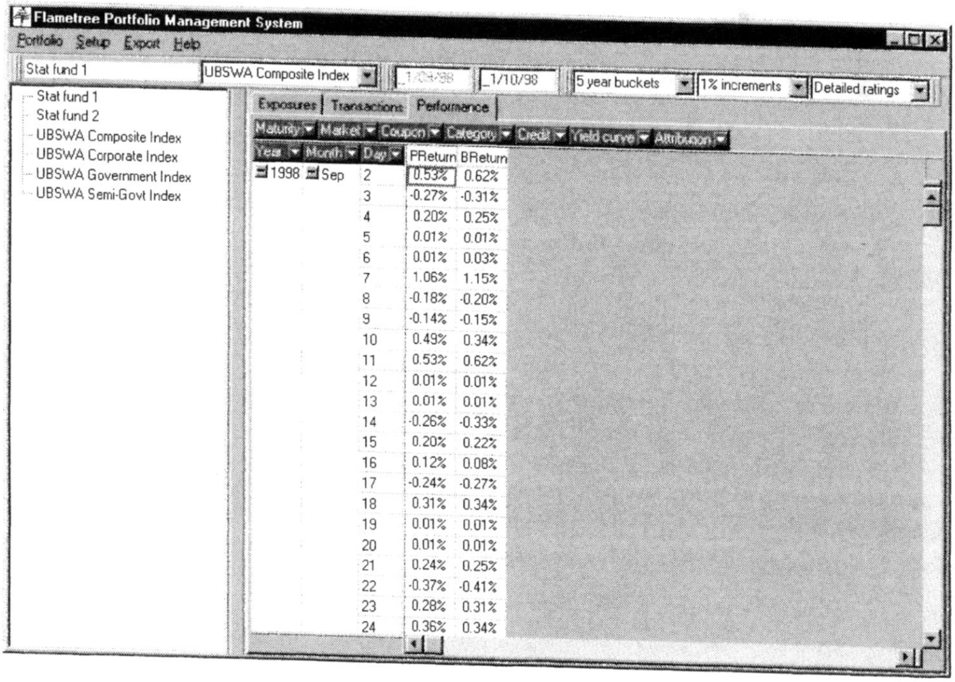

Figure 19.2   Sample OLAP display: performance broken down by date

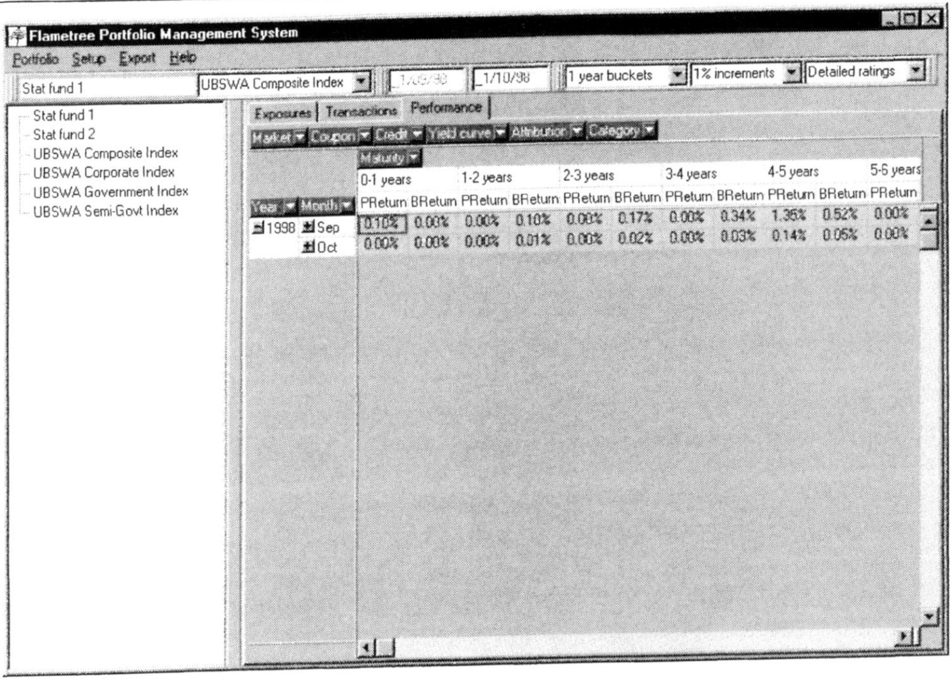

Figure 19.3   Sample OLAP display: performance broken down by maturity bucket

In this framework, attribution becomes just another way to decompose the portfolio's returns. For instance, by using the Attribution box instead of Maturity, the returns are broken down into (Yield return, Curve return, Credit return, Other returns) instead of by maturity bucket (Figure 19.4).

If this decomposition is nested with the Curve effects box, curve return can further be broken down into (Shift return, Twist return, Butterfly return), while credit return can be decomposed into spread returns between various credit curves. In addition, an attribution decomposition can be nested within a conventional decomposition, so that (for instance) one can isolate and rank attribution returns across different credit ratings (Figure 19.5).

This sort of display gets round many of the problems with static reports, whether on paper or on the Web. There are, however, a number of disadvantages with OLAP in its current form. With current OLAP implementations for performance display, the internal aggregation algorithms tend to be rather limited in scope, with most controls supporting only simple sums and differences. This requires some clever programming to get the control to display aggregated returns in the correct manner.

A further issue is that setting up the internal data structures for an OLAP display (known in OLAP terminology as a *cube*) can require substantial amounts of processing power and a large amount of data. This also has implications for the architecture of the system. In Sienna, OLAP aggregation was performed on the client machine, but this is clearly unacceptable for large production systems. In addition, there may be data integrity issues for reporting if part of the return calculation is performed on the client, since in principle the same calculation is being performed at two different points in the system, which brings the possibility of inconsistent results.

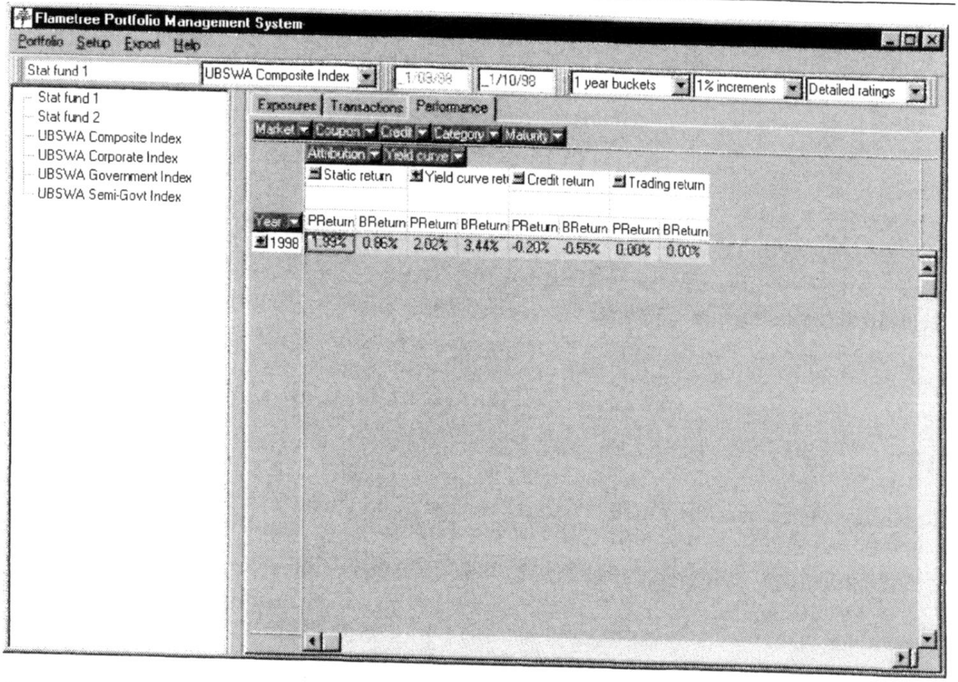

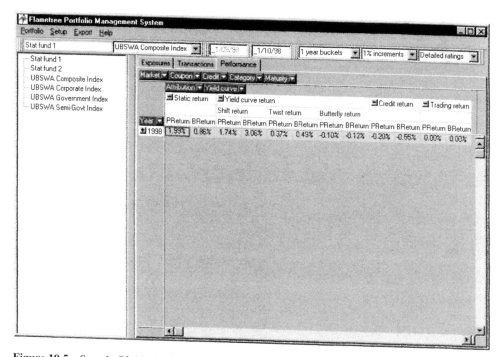

Figure 19.4   Sample OLAP display: performance broken down by summarized attribution effects

Figure 19.5   Sample OLAP display: performance broken down by detailed attribution effects

Despite these issues, the OLAP paradigm was well received. Users became productive with the interface in a very short period of time and were soon producing reports that would normally have taken weeks if they had gone through the usual route of giving the specifications to a programmer.

We expect to see an increase in the use of OLAP-driven displays for presentation of performance and attribution returns over the next few years. Due to the complexity and depth of attribution returns, OLAP has unique advantages for presenting results; its use means the user can choose the level of detail required at the point of delivery, rather than being overwhelmed with information. As with attribution systems generally, progress will be driven by the availability of suitable software.

19.4   PRESENTING GRAPHICAL DATA

Many of the same remarks from the previous section apply to graphical presentation of results.

Consider a portfolio and benchmark with the asset allocations in Table 19.1. For simplicity, we have assumed that the modified durations and yield changes of corresponding buckets within the portfolio and benchmark are the same. In fact this is unlikely to be the case, but it does not affect the argument. Similarly, we have not considered yield return or other effects such as convexity.

From this data, the modified durations of the portfolio and benchmark are 5.58 years and 5.09 years, respectively. The portfolio is therefore 0.49 years long against its benchmark, and is more sensitive overall to interest rate changes than its benchmark. In other words, the manager has positioned the portfolio to benefit from a downwards move in interest rates. Since falling interest rates lead to rising prices, both the portfolio and benchmark will show positive returns if this happens. However, the portfolio has a longer modified duration than the benchmark, so the manager expects the portfolio to rise in value by more than the benchmark, and therefore to show a positive active return.

The yield curve duly falls by an average of 15 basis points. From Equation (7.2), the manager expects to make an active return of

$$-0.49 \times 0.0015 \times 100\% = 74 \text{ basis points}$$

Table 19.1   Asset allocation and risk number for sample portfolio and benchmark

Maturity sector	Portfolio asset allocation (%)	Benchmark asset allocation (%)	Active asset allocation (%)	Modified duration (years)
0–1 years	14	10	4	0.5
1–2 years	17	8	9	1.5
2–3 years	6	12	−6	2.5
3–4 years	10	10	0	3.5
4–5 years	2	9	−7	4.5
5–6 years	3	9	−6	5.5
6–7 years	2	11	−9	6.5
7–8 years	1	10	−9	7.5
8–9 years	5	10	−5	8.5
9–10 years	33	10	23	9.5
>10 years	7	1	6	10.5

Table 19.2 Sample yield curve movement

Maturity sector	Yield curve change (%)
0–1 years	−0.200
1–2 years	−0.200
2–3 years	−0.200
3–4 years	−0.200
4–5 years	−0.200
5–6 years	−0.200
6–7 years	−0.150
7–8 years	−0.150
8–9 years	−0.100
9–10 years	−0.050
>10 years	−0.000
Average	**−0.150**

Unfortunately, the active return turns out to be the substantially different figure of −25 basis points – almost a full percentage point below this expected return. What happened? Let's look at the results in more detail.

The actual yield curve movement is as shown in Table 19.2. The curve has therefore steepened by about 20 basis points. We could describe the curve movement as a twist about the long end of the curve, but it is not necessary to do so in order to analyse the result, which is a major advantage of graphical interpretation.

Firstly, we can graph the asset allocation for portfolio and benchmark to see the *active risk profile*. As Figures 19.6 and 19.7 show, the assets within the portfolio are bunched around the short and long ends of the curve, with relatively low exposures at medium maturities. The benchmark has a relatively uniform distribution of assets across all maturities. This is an example of a bar-bell risk distribution (Figure 19.6).

The active risk allocation can be seen more easily from a graph of the active weights (Figure 19.7). This distribution should give immediate cause for concern if the manager's strategy was to expect a parallel yield curve movement. While the portfolio will benefit from this type of occurrence, it is also extremely vulnerable to other types of curve movement.

Looking deeper at the results, the next step is to look at return contributions by *maturity sector*. Performance contributions are calculated as the product of each sector's active asset allocation and its return. The sum of the performance contributions is the overall active return (Figure 19.8).

This shows that the short and middle ends of the curve added to the portfolio's active return, while the long end lost value. To see the overall contribution of the positive and negative returns, it is useful to graph the results in a different way (Figure 19.9).

Now let's look deeper at the sources of active return. Recall that under the assumptions made at the start of this example, return is generated as the product of the negative modified duration and the change in the sector's yield (Figure 19.10). At the short end, there is a relatively high yield curve movement, but since the modified duration of these instruments is low they are relatively insensitive to interest rate movements, and therefore generate low returns. At the long end of the curve, the curve movement is lowest and so these sectors perform relatively poorly, even though they have the highest interest rate sensitivity.

The sectors with the highest performance lie at the middle of the curve, where the combination of curve movement and modified duration works to greatest advantage.

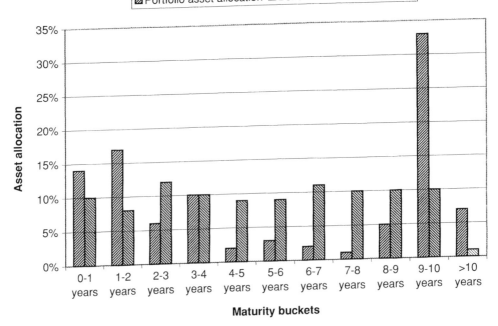

Figure 19.6   Asset allocations for sample portfolio and benchmark

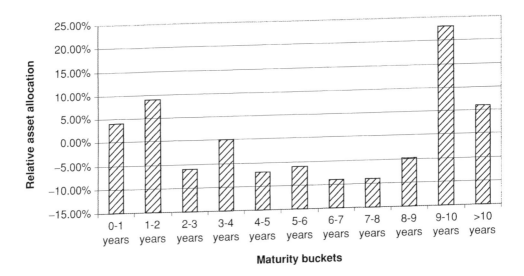

Figure 19.7   Active weights of sample portfolio against benchmark

Performance contribution by maturity bucket

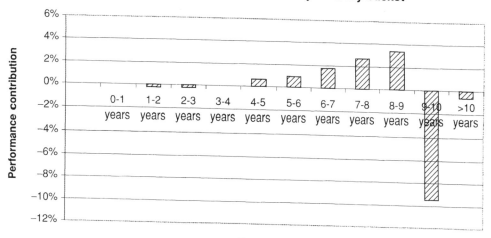

Figure 19.8 Performance contribution against maturity sector

Figure 19.9 Overall positive and negative performance contributions

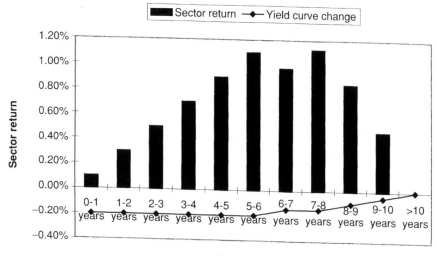

Figure 19.10 Sector return plotted against yield curve change

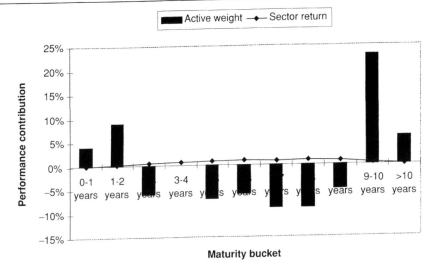

Figure 19.11   Active weight against sector return

The reason for the underperformance should now be clear. Since the benchmark has a relatively uniform distribution of assets across all maturities, a large part of its performance contribution comes from the assets in the middle of the curve. The portfolio, on the other hand, is under-represented at these maturities and so does not stand to benefit from any returns in this area. The result is most clearly seen from a plot of sector return against active weight (Figure 19.11).

What action could the user have taken to stop this happening? The first, and most important, is simply to realize that the position taken, while meeting the stated duration objectives (and probably the portfolio's compliance requirements), carried substantial risks.

In fact, the user stood to benefit from an increase in the yield curve's curvature as well as a decrease in the curve levels. For example, if the curve change in Table 19.2 had occurred, with long and short rates falling by 10 basis points but with intermediate maturities rising by 10 basis points, the portfolio would have outperformed by 43 basis points. Conversely, if long and short rates had risen by 10 basis points with intermediate maturities falling by 10 basis points, a 43 basis point loss would have resulted. In either case, the average movement of the curve is nearly zero, so that a simplistic duration hedging approach would have indicated the profit or loss to be small.

A 10 basis point move in a yield curve across a month is not a large movement. However, a loss of 43 basis points will certainly be noticed!

In practice, a portfolio's active risk profile may well be more complex than this, and it may be necessary to view it at several different levels of resolution in order to gain a true appreciation of the risks in place. As a matter of policy, it is probably still worthwhile examining the expected returns under a group of pre-defined yield curve scenarios, as described in Chapter 17.

This is a deliberately extreme example, in that few fund managers are likely to take this sort of aggressive curve positioning bet without being aware of it. The point of the study is to show the value that graphical displays can add to the interpretation of such results. The key juxtaposition is between the graphs in Figures 19.10 and 19.11, comparing active weight to the sector returns generated by yield curve movements.

19.5   REPORT DESIGN

There is ample scope for the user to add value to reports through good design. For instance, to indicate the relationship between yield change, modified duration and sector weight on performance contribution, one might set up a graph in which each maturity bucket displays a rectangle with width equal to the modified duration of the bucket, and height equal to the change in yield. The height of the boxes across all maturities therefore graphs the change in the yield curve, while the area of the box shows the performance contribution due to yield changes. Adding the areas of the boxes together gives the total performance of the portfolio.

Regarding numerical reports, there is also scope to introduce interactive graphical displays. The user may well find interpretation of results easier if he can click on a part of a graph and have it opened up in more detail. For instance, if a risk graph shows an unexpectedly high concentration of assets in one maturity bucket, it may be useful to click on that bucket and examine the individual securities within. Similarly, the fastest way to see the causes of a portfolio's performance may be to start at relatively large maturity buckets of (say) 5 years width, drill down to buckets of 1 year, then to individual securities, and even to individual cash flows if required.

In the author's view, the role of good graphical design in presentation of attribution returns has been grossly underestimated. There is ample scope to add value to attribution reporting systems through ergonomically designed, easy to interpret reports. Some good sources of ideas on data presentation and user interface design may be found in Tufte (1990), Cooper (1995) and Norman (1990).

Beyond Fixed Income Attribution

20.1 FIXED INCOME ATTRIBUTION IN THE INVESTMENT PROCESS

What happens when you have attribution reporting up and running? It is worth giving this question some consideration, since the ability to run attribution will inevitably bring a host of changes in its wake.

Attribution may initially prove to be a double-edged sword due to its ability to show embarrassing gaps in the hedging abilities of many fund managers. Do not be surprised to see purchases of attribution systems being followed relatively promptly by purchases of advanced risk management and portfolio optimization software. The end results will certainly justify the costs, both in terms of improving fund returns, and in transparency and marketability of the fund's products. In the short term, though, putting in an attribution capability will inevitably lead to further expenditure on investment technology. Be warned!

In addition, the ability to carry out attribution is likely to make a substantial impact on the *investment process* of many fund managers. Investment process is the fund's sequence of research, modelling, forming judgements, allocation of risk, continuing risk management and portfolio construction. Attribution allows the introduction of feedback into risk management and portfolio construction, so that the success – or otherwise – of all investment decisions can be assessed and the portfolio structure amended accordingly. As managers identify the benefits that attribution can make, they will call for better tools for risk hedging and portfolio optimization, and probably more frequent performance and attribution reporting – and that's just to start.

In the author's view, the process requirements and tools described below will become indispensable fixed income portfolio management tools, once attribution is widely in use.

20.1.1 Improved term structure modelling

The ability to assess the impact of yield curve movements, in detail, will require managers to move beyond a simplistic duration hedging approach. A clearly articulated view of yield curve and credit spread movements will be vital for effective curve movement hedging.

Of course, this is not always possible. A manager may have a rough idea of how term structure changes may develop, but may not be able to articulate a more precise opinion. We may therefore see the development of *fuzzy decision systems* (Kosko, 1992; Cox, 1995) to assist in describing future term structure movements. Such systems allow users to express views in ways that are imprecise but can be interpreted and used by decision systems.

For instance, a curve view may be expressed in the form

Sovereign curve will show a SMALL move upwards at SHORT maturities
Sovereign curve will show a MODERATE move upwards at INTERMEDIATE maturities
Sovereign curve will show a MODERATE move upwards at LONG maturities

Table 20.1   Probabilities of curve movement types

Sovereign curve movement	Probability (%)
Unchanged	50
Slight steepening	20
Major steepening	10
Slight flattening	10
Major flattening	10

Table 20.2   Probabilities of credit spread movements

Credit spreads
Unchanged: 30%
Increase: 50%
Decrease: 20%

and

> Credit curve will show a LARGE contraction at SHORT maturities
> Credit curve will show a LARGE contraction at INTERMEDIATE maturities
> Credit curve will show a MODERATE contraction at LONG maturities

where the adjectives (SMALL, MODERATE, LARGE, SHORT, INTERMEDIATE, LONG) are all fuzzy variables.

Similarly, the manager may feel that several scenarios are likely to occur, with varying degrees of likelihood (see Tables 20.1 and 20.2).

Here the risk assessment is tailored to the manager's view of the term structure, in that no curvature movements of the sovereign curve are considered, and no fine structure in the credit spread is considered. A sophisticated risk assessment tool will accept such limited inputs and combine them with the current active exposures of the benchmark. One such technique is Saaty's analytical hierarchy process (AHP), which allows decisions to be made up from hierarchies of weighted, sometimes contradictory judgements and rankings, expressed in numerical form or as relative value judgements (Saaty, 1988; Colin, 1999).

Since no views on some types of curve movement are expressed, the risk tool should try to hedge against changes in these types of movement so that active returns are unaffected. Of course, this may not always be possible, in which case the tool should either do the best it can, or inform the user and request fresh instructions.

20.1.2   Risk and reward

With such views of risk available, it becomes possible to assess the range of outcomes for the portfolio, and this may affect the active risk taken. For instance, one fund manager may adopt a risk position that leads to a moderate gain with 60% probability, but a major loss with 5% probability. For another manager, this risk profile may be unacceptable, and they will hedge the portfolio in a different way so as to remove the potential major loss, even if this lessens the expected moderate gain. The manager's appetite for risk will probably be set by company policy or investor mandate.

To quantify the portfolio's expected risks and returns in this way may require a combination of Value at Risk (VaR) tools (Butler, 1999) and risk modelling techniques. Beforehand, however, the manager must articulate what this risk strategy actually is.

20.1.3   What-if risk modelling

An important tool to assess the likely outcomes of various investment strategies are what-if modelling tools. These work by imposing various changes on the shape of the yield curves that drive the performance of the portfolio and benchmark over a given period into the future, and then calculating the resulting active performance under the effects of these changes. What-if modelling can be run in the following way.

1. Manually changing the shape of the curves, and examining the effect on active return. This is useful for informal discussion and strategic planning. However, it is important to ensure that no curve movement types have been omitted. This type of analysis is best run in conjunction with formal analyses of sets of pre-defined curve movements.
2. Use of suites of pre-defined yield curve change scenarios. In this approach, the user sets up suites of expected curve movements similar to those shown above.
3. Monte Carlo modelling and simulation. Monte Carlo modelling assumes that interest rates can be described as a stochastic process, or that they move randomly under certain constraints. The current shape of the yield curve is then modified by various random influences over a given simulation period, so that the shape of the curve at the end of the period reflects one possible outcome. The performances of the portfolio and benchmark are then calculated using this modified yield curve. The process is then repeated several thousand times and the distribution of active returns is calculated.

Monte Carlo simulation can be a remarkably powerful tool if the dynamics of the underlying processes are properly understood. It has the disadvantage that simulation can be very computer-intensive, although techniques such as use of antithetic variables and variance reduction can improve the speed of simulations (see Press *et al.*, 1992 for more information).

20.1.4   Portfolio optimizers

Changing the risk profile of a portfolio in response to changing market conditions is frequently one of the most time-consuming parts of managing a portfolio. Modifying the active exposure of a portfolio is a complex and demanding task, particularly when we take into account:

- maintenance of the overall structure of a portfolio;
- compliance rules should not be breached or will not be breached in the face of likely future market changes;
- minimum deal sizes;
- minimization of dealing costs.

There are numerous mathematical techniques for dealing with such optimization problems, including linear and integer programming, simulated annealing, genetic algorithms, and many others.

20.1.5   Systems integration

In practice, these tools will not – and should not – be used in isolation. All the tools we have described need to be able to recover the current holdings in the portfolio and its benchmark, risk numbers for all securities or sectors, and the current state of the market's yield curves. This suggests the use of a common platform for data storage.

The user will then iterate around the risk/positioning/optimization loop several times until a set of portfolio adjustments has been found that meets all criteria as closely as possible. It is probably unrealistic to expect every constraint to be met. Instead, the manager will have to make a series of informed decisions about how far to take the optimization process in the light of their tolerance for risk and the perceived likelihood of various market movements. We can therefore expect to see more of a convergence of front-, middle- and back-office functions.

20.2   CONCLUSION

There exists huge potential to boost fixed income portfolio returns by judicious use of technology. In fact, the complexity of fixed income risk and performance analysis is such that there is no option but to turn to such tools. Attribution is just the first step on this route.

Yet, as with all investment problems, the answer is not only to be found in the use of computer programs; there will always remain a vital role for human judgement and skill. The virtue of the various tools and processes suggested above is that they free up the user to exercise these skills. The clarity and insight brought by adding attribution to this process is only the first step.

Derivation of the Normal Equations for a Least Squares Fit

A.1 POLYNOMIAL FUNCTIONS

For a polynomial function, the yield points are assumed to fit the relationship

$$y(t) = a_0 + a_1 t + a_2 t^2 \tag{A.1}$$

where there are n sets of values for $(t, y(t))$.

If we know the values of t and $y(t)$, there are several equations we can derive from this expression. Firstly, sum the expression over all sample points. This will give

$$\sum y = \sum a_0 + \sum a_1 t + \sum a_2 t^2 \tag{A.2}$$

Rearranging, this gives

$$\sum y = a_0 \cdot n + a_1 \sum t + a_2 \sum t^2 \tag{A.3}$$

Next, multiply the base expression by t and sum over all terms to give

$$\sum y \cdot t = a_0 \sum t + a_1 \sum t^2 + a_2 \sum t^3 \tag{A.4}$$

Lastly, multiply the base expression by y and sum over all terms to give

$$\sum y^2 = a_0 \sum y + a_1 \sum y \cdot t + a_2 \sum y \cdot t^2 \tag{A.5}$$

These three equations (known as the normal equations) are in three unknowns (a_0, a_1, a_2) and may be solved simultaneously as a matrix equation to give values for (a_0, a_1, a_2):

$$\begin{pmatrix} n & \sum t & \sum t^2 \\ \sum t & \sum t^2 & \sum t^3 \\ \sum y & \sum y \cdot t & \sum y \cdot t^2 \end{pmatrix} \begin{pmatrix} a_0 \\ a_1 \\ a_2 \end{pmatrix} = \begin{pmatrix} \sum y \\ \sum y \cdot t \\ \sum y^2 \end{pmatrix} \tag{A.6}$$

A.2 NELSON–SIEGEL FUNCTIONS

A Nelson–Siegel function has the form

$$R(m) = \beta + (\beta_1 + \beta_2) \frac{\left[1 - \exp\left(-\dfrac{m}{\tau}\right)\right]}{\left(\dfrac{m}{\tau}\right)} - \beta_2 \exp\left(-\dfrac{m}{\tau}\right) \tag{A.7}$$

Rewriting Equation (A.7) and grouping coefficients, the yield points fit the function

$$y(t) = \beta_0 + \beta_1 \left(\frac{1 - \exp(-t)}{t}\right) + \beta_2 \left[\left(\frac{1 - \exp(-t)}{t}\right) - \exp(-t)\right] \tag{A.8}$$

where t has been rescaled to meet the requirements of the user.

Defining the quantities

$$X(t) = \frac{1 - \exp(-t)}{t} \tag{A.9}$$

and

$$Y(t) = \frac{1 - \exp(-t)}{t} - \exp(-t) = X(t) - \exp(-t) \tag{A.10}$$

the Nelson–Siegel function becomes

$$y(t) = \beta_0 + \beta_1 \cdot X(t) + \beta_2 \cdot Y(t) \tag{A.11}$$

In this case, the normal equations become

$$\begin{pmatrix} n & \sum X(t) & \sum Y(t) \\ \sum X(t) & \sum X(t)^2 & \sum X(t) \cdot Y(t) \\ \sum Y(t) & \sum X(t) \cdot Y(t) & \sum Y(t)^2 \end{pmatrix} \begin{pmatrix} \beta_0 \\ \beta_1 \\ \beta_2 \end{pmatrix} = \begin{pmatrix} \sum y(t) \\ \sum y(t) \cdot X(t) \\ \sum y(t) \cdot Y(t) \end{pmatrix} \tag{A.12}$$

Note that, in some circumstances, direct use of the normal equations can lead to rounding errors. A more robust fitting algorithm is singular value decomposition, which is covered in Press *et al.* (1992, chap. 15).

References

Anderson, N., Breedon, F., Deacon, M., Derry, A., Murphy, G., *Estimating and Interpreting the Yield Curve*, John Wiley & Sons, Ltd, 1996, pp. 20–48.

Bacon, C., *Practical Portfolio Performance Measurement and Attribution*, John Wiley & Sons, Ltd, 2004.

Barber, J.R., Copper, M.L., 'Immunization using principal component analysis', *Journal of Portfolio Management*, Fall, 1996.

Bolder, D., Streliski, D., 'Yield curve modeling at the Bank of Canada', Technical Report no. 84, Bank of Canada, February, 1999 (available at http://www.bankofcanada.ca/en/res/tr84-e.htm).

Bonafede, J.K., Foresti, S.J., Matheos, P., 'A multi-period linking algorithm that has stood the test of time', *Journal of Performance Measurement*, Fall, 2002.

Brinson, G.P., Fachler, N., 'Measuring non-US equity portfolio performance', *Journal of Portfolio Management*, Spring, 1985.

Brooks, F.P., *The Mythical Man-Month*, Addison-Wesley, 1975.

Burnie, J.S., Knowles, J.A., Teder, T.J., 'Arithmetic and geometric attribution', *Journal of Performance Measurement*, Fall, 1998.

Butler, C., *Mastering Value at Risk*, Prentice-Hall, 1999.

Cariño, D.R., 'Combining attribution effects over time', *Journal of Performance Measurement*, Summer, 1999.

Cariño, D.R., 'Refinements in multi-period attribution', *Journal of Performance Measurement*, Fall, 2002.

Choudhry, M., *Analysing and Interpreting the Yield Curve*, John Wiley & Sons, 2004.

Colin, A.M., 'The analytic hierarchy process', *Dr Dobb's Journal*, February, 1999.

Cooper, A., *About Face: The Essentials of User Interface Design*, IDG Books, 1995.

Cox, E.D., *Fuzzy Logic for Business and Industry*, Charles River, 1995.

Dietz, P.O., *Pension Funds: Measuring Investment Performance*, The Free Press, 1966.

Elton, E.J., Gruber, M.J., *Modern Portfolio Theory and Investment Analysis*, John Wiley & Sons, Inc, 1995.

Frongello, A.S.B., 'Attribution linking: proofed and clarified', *Journal of Performance Measurement*, Fall, 2002.

Hayre, L. (ed.), *Salomon Smith Barney Guide to Mortgage-Backed and Asset-Backed Securities*, John Wiley & Sons, Inc, 2001.

J.P. Morgan, 'Government Bond Outlines', New York and London, 2001.

Kahn, R.N., 'Bond performance analysis: a multi-factor approach', *Journal of Portfolio Management*, Fall, 1991.

Karnosky, S.K., Singer, B.D., *Global Asset Management and Performance Attribution*, Blackwell, 2000.

Kline, K., Gould, L., Zanevsky, A., *Transact-SQL Programming*, O'Reilly, 1999.

Kosko, B., *Neural Networks and Fuzzy Systems: A Dynamical Systems Approach to Machine Intelligence*, Prentice-Hall, 1992.

Laker, D., 'What is this thing called interaction?', *Journal of Performance Measurement*, Fall, 2000.

Liang, B., 'Price pressure: evidence from the "Dartboard" column', *Journal of Business, Chicago*, **72**(1), 1999, 119–135.

Nelson, C.R., Siegel, A.F., 'Parsimonious modeling of yield curves', *Journal of Business*, **60**(4), 1987, 473–489.

Norman, D.A., *The Design of Everyday Things*, Doubleday, 1990.

Press, W.H., Teukolsky, S.A., Vetterling, W.T., Flannery, B.P., *Numerical Recipes in C*, Cambridge University Press, 1992.

Saaty, T.L., *Mathematical Methods of Operational Research*, Dover, 1988.

Singer, D.S., Gonzalo, M., Lederman, M., 'Multi-period attribution: residuals and compounding', *Journal of Performance Measurement*, Fall, 1998.

Spaulding, D., 'Demystifying the interaction effect', *Journal of Performance Measurement*, Winter, 2003a.

Spaulding, D., *Investment Performance Attribution*, McGraw-Hill, 2003b.

Tritsch, S., 'Bull marketing', *Chicago Magazine*, March, 1998.

Tufte, E.R., *Envisioning Information*, Graphics Press, 1990.

Index

Index compiled by Annette Musker

Printed in the USA/Agawam, MA
December 13, 2013

583055.071